MEMOIRS OF AN AFRICAN WOMAN ON A MISSION

MEMOIRS OF AN AFRICAN WOMAN ON A MISSION

OLEY DIBBA-WADDA

Dedication

My memoirs are dedicated
to the African woman and the African girl child,
without whom my purpose and passion in life
—*to give ALL that I have and ALL that I AM*—
would be worthless.

In memory of Aunty Mama and Dad.
Your presence continues to be felt
in everything I think, do, and say.
Your spirits live on.

My God, I give you ALL the glory!

Table of Contents

INTRODUCTION   1

UNUSUAL BEGINNINGS   3

MEMBERS OF THE CLAN   12

AUNTY MAMA   19

BURNS AND SCARS   29

BREAKING THE RULES   33

BIRD SET FREE   39

EXPECTED OF A WIFE   53

ABANDONED IN MARRIAGE   61

YEARNING FOR THE UNKNOWN   65

THE MORE I RECEIVED   71

IT WAS THE DAY   78

MY COURTSHIP WITH ABUNDANCE   86

QUEST FOR LIFE'S PURPOSE   96

WHEN THE KNOWING EMERGED   106

TAMING THE BEAST   114

IN LOVE WITH GRATITUDE   122

IT IS MY DESIRE   128

EPILOGUE   132

ACKNOWLEDGMENTS   142

ABOUT THE AUTHOR   143

INTRODUCTION

Around my forty-fifth birthday, a colleague asked me, "So, Oley, what is next for you? Where do you see yourself in five years' time? You have practically ticked almost all your boxes, an unusual combination of achievements for you as a woman at forty-five years old."

"What do you mean?" I asked.

He responded, "At age forty-five, you have reached the highest academic achievement." At the time I was still in my third year as a Doctoral student. "At forty-five," he continued, "You have reached the highest position as CEO of a Pan African Organization. At forty-five you have reached the highest voluntary position as Chair of Board of Trustees. You are still married, not divorced or widowed, with a loving husband who would support you wherever you go. You have four children."

And he went on. "At forty-five you have travelled to more than fifty countries around the world across five continents. You continue to mentor, coach, inspire, motivate and act as a role model to a lot of youths, particularly young African girls and you have not clocked fifty years yet. So . . . what's next?" he asked.

At forty-five I didn't have a response for his question.

It was the first time I had been presented with a series of my own life's events like that. I had actually not thought of what was next until he asked the question. Over the past years I have met a lot of people, through my work and socially, who felt inspired by what I do, what I stand for and, I guess, who I am and what I aspire to be. Young women and girls I come across in my work often say to me, "I want to be like you when I grow up," and "You are truly an inspiration to me." And they ask, "How did you get to where you are? What did you have to do to get there?"

Questions, questions and more questions over the years. These questions prompted me to have deep conversations with myself to find the answers. The process helped me appreciate how far I have come.

I came to realise, and what I know now, is that I had to go through the experiences of my journey to get to where I am today, that everything that happened to me was life teaching me and preparing me for my growth. I have become aware, I've accepted and acknowledged life's lessons. I understand and appreciate the people who crossed my path for a reason, a season, and a lifetime. I discovered that the issues I held against others and myself were eating me up—and only me—on the inside. I learned that I had to forgive myself and everyone else for several misunderstandings during adolescence. I learned that I needed to heal on the inside.

Embracing these life lessons helped me discover myself, and in the process I not only found my purpose, but I also opened myself up to the abundance of blessings that had been there waiting for me all the while. Because of these lessons I have made the decision to share my journey. It is my desire to share my stories so that others who may be going through some of these similar experiences may wish to revisit their reaction to life's lessons and blessings. These are the stories I share through my memoirs . . . Memoirs of an African woman on a mission.

UNUSUAL BEGINNINGS

Given my current spiritual growth and awareness, it is no co-incidence that I am inspired to start writing this book today. It is 9 September 2016, here in Ivory Coast, Abidjan. I am sitting on my bed whilst my husband Bye Malleh, whom I have been married to for twenty-three years now, lies next to me sleeping. I decided to work from home today. I slept in late, made myself some coffee and signed in on my work computer. As I checked my business emails, sent a couple of emails to colleagues in the office and made a few phone calls, I kept noticing the date on my calendar.

Today's date magnified this day's significance.

It was fifty years ago today when my parents got married and started their life together. Forty-four years ago today my youngest sister, Lu, was born. And today my only daughter, Katty, who is twenty-one years of age, moves into her own studio for the first time. As I have become more and more in tune with my inner self and more open to my intuition, these signs have become more pronounced and not so subtle anymore.

Today is a day of new beginnings, a day to celebrate life's journeys, a day to launch a new venture of my own. As I sit leaning against a pile of pillows on my bed with my computer propped in my lap, I begin to write . . .

I was born on 24 March 1967 to my father, Omar Baboucar Yusupha Dibba, and my mother, Lucretia Eleanor Clara

Dibba (nee Carayol), in the United Kingdom at the Churchill Hospital in Oxford. As their eldest child I was named after my dad's mother, Oley, and also given my mother's middle names, Lucretia Clara.

My parents had married in the United Kingdom a year earlier. They rented a small room at 89 Iffley Road in Oxford, living off the scholarship stipend awarded by the British Council for my father to attend the university. Many bright young Gambian men, like my dad, were chosen to study abroad with the expectations of returning home to invest fresh knowledge into the homeland.

My ambitious father studied Economics at Wadham College, Oxford University on a British Council scholarship. Prior, he attended Fourahbay College (FBC) in Sierra Leone attaining the second highest score and earning a transfer to the Durham University in the United Kingdom (at the time FBC was twinned with Durham University), where he studied Political Science.

Mum relocated to the UK as a teenager. Although her parents had been residing and working in the UK for some time, my mum had been living in The Gambia with her grand aunt, Mrs. Lucretia, Ayeshemi St Clair Joof (nee Lusack). She attended St. Joseph's High School, a Catholic girls' high school managed by Irish nuns. I would later go to the same high school myself. Mum's parents decided she should complete her education in the United Kingdom. Three days before Christmas in 1965, the same year the small country of The Gambia gained its independence from the British Empire, Mum travelled to the UK to join her mum and stepfather. She continued her education at the Hammersmith College in Brookgreen in London and married my father shortly after graduation.

Coincidentally, Mum and Dad had lived on the same street in their home country, not far from each other. It was fitting, perhaps meaningful, that the street was named Perseverance Street.

I recall stories from both Mum and Dad how life was for them in the UK with a child. In addition to his studies, Dad carried the responsibility of supporting his new Gambian wife and baby daughter, spending most of his stipend for living expenses. They would explain how they had to live off tins of Pilchards (sardine-like fish with tomato sauce) and rice. Both my parents say I was a very calm and quiet baby. Hardly ever cried, even when I was hungry. Mum would say how sometimes she forgot that it was my feeding time because I did not cry or fuss. Rather, I would lie still where I was placed without a worry in the world. Looking back now, this seems ironic, considering the turbulent behavior that I would display in years to come.

After my dad completed his studies in the UK, we returned to The Gambia. I was told we sailed from the United Kingdom to The Gambia on a ship named Apapa. The journey took weeks. My mother explained how they were so poor that she landed in The Gambia with her wedding dress, a simple, white, sleeveless, knee-length, laced dress, as that was the best she had at the time. My father took a job as a public servant with the government of The Gambia, first as a Commissioner in the Western Division of The Gambia, then was identified amongst other young Gambians to be part of the transition team to secure the Central Bank of The Gambia as solely owned and managed by Gambians. He later worked in the insurance business and became the first Gambian Managing Director of The Gambia National Insurance Corporation.

During the next five years, three siblings joined me—Penda, and Omar Junior (whom we referred to as Omey), and Lucretia, (referred to as Lu). My younger siblings were all born in The Gambia. I was the only one who had been born in the UK, an unusual beginning that would prove remarkable many years later.

For young parents with four children living in Africa in the 1960s and 1970s, life was not easy, as both my parents would remind us. In early 1970, Dad joined the United Nations Economic Commission for Africa (UNECA) in Addis Ababa, Ethiopia, where we lived for two years.

When our family returned to The Gambia from Ethiopia in 1972, we moved into an unfinished house on 2 December

1972 on the day Dad turned thirty-two years of age. I was six years old. My father had acquired land in the Fajara area of The Gambia, a zone that at the time was allocated mostly for Gambian professionals, like my father, who were returning home from further studies.

I have memories of growing up in that house; some good, and some not so good.

When we moved into the unfinished house, the walls of the house were not yet painted and sand was piled up in what would later be the living room. The kitchen was not ready and neither were the bedrooms. The building was dark and grey. In the beginning, my parents slept in their uncompleted bedroom while my siblings and I slept in what later became my parents' dressing room. During the day, our house helps would take the charcoal pots and utensils to cook and clean outside. In the evenings, they would bring everything back inside. A few fruit trees were planted outside—avocado, mango, lime and banana trees—around the huge compound.

During that period, people acquired vast plots of land for residential purposes. At the time not many people lived in our neighborhood. There were no streetlights or tar roads. The sandy road was a ten-minute walk down the Fajara beach and a five-minute walk to the Fajara Golf Course and the Fajara Hotel. On the other side of Fajara, where our house was situated, lived some of the older professionals. Most were from the *Aku* and Catholic communities, with a few Muslim professionals scattered around different parts of the Fajara neighbourhood.

Aku was the name given for the Christian families (from the Methodist and Anglican churches), who were descendants of the slaves who had been returned back to The Gambia. Gathered from the United States and the United Kingdom, the freed slaves were dropped off in Liberia and Sierra Leone. The *Aku* and Catholic families also included those who were of mixed race, the offspring of white men who came to The Gambia to settle and had children with black African women. My completely white great-great-great-grandfather Jean Carayol migrated to The Gambia from France with two other siblings during the Napoleon era to escape the war. They were from an aristocratic family and were trying to protect their thriving businesses outside of France. The three brothers migrated to West Africa; two settled in The Gambia and one in neighbouring Senegal. My great-grandfather had a son with a local Muslim woman named Jorjoh Jow. Thus, my grandfather and his offspring, my mum included, were referred to as Mulattos (*Malatarr* as pronounced in the *Wolof* dialect).

My Mulatto mother came from an affluent family. Some members of her family had held key positions—for the prison services, magistrate and the judiciary, politicians—in The Gambia and were influential as public servants. In addition, there seems to have been an elevated status given to professional *Aku*, Catholic and Mulatto families at the time.

Most of the older professionals owned properties right next to the seaside or the golf course in Fajara. The neighborhood was one of the prime residential neighborhoods and anyone who acquired a property in that area (usually allocated by the government) typically had the privilege of graduating with a degree as a doctor, lawyer, dentist, engineer, economist or other, outside of The Gambia and returned home to serve his country or held a recognized position working in his home country. I say "his" because during that period of African history, land was mostly acquired by men.

Over the years my parents continued to extend the building and had managed to split the compound into three different properties, with us living in the main property. Eventually Mum and Dad had a study room, a master bedroom, a dressing room and private toilet and bath within the house. Each of my three siblings and I had our own rooms, but shared a bath and toilet. We referred to the living room and family room as the verandah (still do) because of the way it was built—open with lots of windows. As kids we spent most of our time playing with our toys in the verandah. Then there was the dining room, an inside and an outside kitchen, and a garage. In those days, we had quarters for the maids (house help) who slept with us during the week, went home on Saturday evening to spend time with their families, and returned to our house on Monday morning. These quarters were built outside of the main house but within the compound. We grew up having two maids, a gardener, a driver, and a night watchman who lived in the compound with his family permanently.

My parents had a craving for building and construction work. Actually, it was more my mum than my dad. Mum was the one "addicted to cement and sand." Her interests were ones mostly assigned for men. And this was just something she loved and enjoyed. Mum was the one who changed the light bulbs in the house. She was the one who hung paintings on the wall with nails and hammers and climbing on ladders. If Dad were around, he would sit on his favorite dedicated chair and give instructions for Mum to shift slightly to the right or to the left to find the perfect spot to hit the nail on the wall and hang the photos.

Mum also had a thing for plants and flowers. People used to come to our house just to visit Mum's garden or to ask for some seedlings to replant in their own gardens. On her travels with Dad, Mum would return back home with cuttings from plants. We had the most exotic plants and flowers in our garden. Mum was so devoted to her plants that she would wake up at five o'clock every morning to water her plants herself, talk to them, even crush aspirin (medical tablets) mixed with water to give some of her plants when she felt they were not doing well or under the weather. Mum would literally spend all the money she had on cement, sand, building materials, plants and flowerpots. For Gambian women in those days, this was not common. Gambian women focused mostly on their external appearances, on ceremonies, cooking, trading businesses, and their home and so on; a few had interests in plants but not to the extent Mum was. These were her passions, her hobbies. She was not one to do much cooking. Once in a while she would cook, but not often. Mum followed her passions, and I learned quickly to try to not get in her way.

Mum made me start taking on kitchen chores and going to the market as soon as I started high school, at the age of eleven.

She required I take an inventory of the fresh produce in the kitchen pantry and the refrigerator, listing the ones that had run out. She'd then explain how much of what vegetables we should buy. Toting the market-shopping basket that was almost my size, I would take a taxi about twenty minutes' drive away to the nearest produce market. On my way back, I struggled to carry the heavy basket of produce; sometimes it did not all fit in the basket, and I had to carry the excess in plastic carrier bags. I'd drag myself to the house from the junction of our street where the taxi drivers would usually drop us off.

When Penda was a little older, Mum enrolled her in the market chores as well. We followed the same process we used for produce for our other groceries. After a thorough inventory, we would go shopping at the CFAO main supermarket in Bakau, at the time one of the largest supermarkets in The Gambia. At the CFAO supermarket, we would get fresh dairy products like butter, cheese, milk and eggs as well as fresh bread and other perishables, again enough to last for the week.

Mum believed in bulk shopping. At the end of each month, we would go with her to purchase wholesale supplies like detergents, bags of sugar, bags of rice, cartons or drums of oil, cartons of tomato pastes and so on. Our home had two pantries. The large pantry, which we used to call "the store," was actually set up like a shop similar to the corner convenience stores in most neighborhoods. Mum built shelves on the wall and we would display the items on the shelves as if they were for sale, lining up the produce in order of the date purchased. Last in, first out. LIFO. As we grew older and stronger, the main grocery and bulk shopping chores were also transferred to my sister and me.

Then came the cooking. When the maids took the weekends off, my sister Penda and I were responsible to cook for the family on Sundays. We had to wake up early on Sunday mornings to prepare breakfast, which meant no opportunity to have a lay in during the weekends. We had to prepare lunch and dinner also. If the food was too salty, or the sauce too watery the slippers would be on my back.

Sold locally, the slippers were made of a rubber texture with white soles, and came mostly in white and green colours on the straps. The slippers were the easiest ammunition for Mum; all she had to do was remove them from her feet when there was nothing else around to use on me. She would ask a question about why the mistake happened, whatever it was, with a slipper on one foot and the other in her hand, raised and about to strike.

As I tried to explain, I would still get beaten. She would say, "So you are answering me back?"

But then when I didn't respond and bowed my head down so our eyes would not meet, she would say, "So I ask you a question and you have decided not to respond?"

There was no escaping. When that slipper left the foot, it had to strike whether I responded or not, whether I tried to explain or not.

My sister and I would usually rotate our chores. On weekends I was responsible for the kitchen she would be responsible for cleaning the house. We would sweep the entire house and all the rooms, change all the bed linens, wash the bathroom and toilets, and polish the furniture. Our duties for preparing breakfast, lunch and dinner involved tidying the kitchen and dining areas, setting the table, washing the refrigerator and doing the dishes. God help us if the table was not set up properly, or the dishes not properly cleaned (there were no washing machines then) or worse, we did not bring the right change home from the market. Mum would make me calculate the cost of every item bought from the market. If it did not tally with the amount of money she had given me, her slippers would be on my back and all over me. There were times when I had to take my weekly pocket money to pay Mum back when I was shortchanged at the market; otherwise, I would be in trouble.

Every Sunday, it was also the responsibility of the person who was doing the kitchen to take out detergents, sugar and rice, etc., from the pantry for the week's stock and organise them in the smaller pantry inside the kitchen. The main pantry was always under lock and key and was only opened on Sundays for replenishment for the following week.

Mum also had a thing for packing and tidying, repacking and straightening up linen closets, dining room cupboards, etc. All the hangers in the wardrobe had to have the mouth face inwards. Similarly, the toilet roll. It had to be placed in the holder with the sheet being able to be pulled from the top rather than from underneath. Towels on the rack had to be matching. Curtains hung had a special way of being hooked on the runners. If they were not done the right way, the slippers, if we were lucky, would be on us or if we were unlucky it could be worse—branches from the Causaurina plant—or even worse, Dad's belt. It was the same for changing the sheets and making the beds. There were five beds that had to be changed, using a fitted sheet, a straight sheet and a bed cover. It was as if one was working as a chambermaid in a hotel.

We did not like it at the time when Mum insisted we learned to cook and cleanup and tidy the house, especially when we had two maids, but if there was one thing my sisters and I learned from Mum, it was how to run and manage a perfect home later in life. Today, Penda and I have taken these same examples running our homes the same way, entertaining the same way, shopping the same way including bulk shopping for the month. I run my own home the same way as Mum taught us. Minus the slippers.

As I mentioned, Mum didn't cook much, but she taught me how to cook all the local and traditional meals that are cooked in my country. It is a pride I carry with me today; although, I must confess that I married a man who equally loves to cook and entertain. As a result, like Mum, I seldom cook, only if and when we are entertaining. We usually have house help and chefs who are responsible for the cooking anyway, but when either of us, my husband or I, are in the mood to cook, we could spend the whole day in the kitchen. Given my background in the kitchen, on those occasions when I do decide to be the chef for the day, I like to have everything pre prepped, my *mise en place* all prepared and lined up ready to go into the cooking pots and saucepans.

MEMBERS OF THE CLAN

My mother was *Aku* because her mother, Abie Belle, hailed from the *Aku* tribe, but she was Catholic by birth because her father, Ernest Carayol, was Catholic. She was baptized and had her Holy First Communion as a young Catholic girl, attended a Catholic primary school and Catholic high school. She later became a Methodist after she married my dad in the UK and they returned to The Gambia. The Catholic Church during that period would only allow her to take Holy Communion if both she and her husband agreed for the church to bless their union. Both of my parents did not agree to that condition. My father was a Muslim.

Neither of my parents converted. They both maintained their religions and as a result my siblings and I were raised acknowledging and celebrating Christmas, Easter, the two Muslim celebrations of Eid, and the holy month of Ramadan. During Ramadan, my mum would fast throughout the month to support my dad, and during the festive Christmas holidays my dad would play the piano as we sang Christmas hymns at home. My dad also went to a Methodist Boys' High School and later to college in Sierra Leone before going to the university in the United Kingdom.

Because he attended a Methodist school and spent time in Sierra Leone, where the creole *Aku* dialect (Pidgeon English) was spoken, it was easy for him to communicate with my mum. We all spoke the *Aku* dialect at home. Mum could speak and understand the *Wolof* dialect, which was my dad's mother tongue, but she was not very fluent in it at the time. I believe I was more fluent in both languages because of my influences outside of the home. I also went to a Methodist primary school and a Catholic Girls' High school.

Mum inherited from her grandmother quite a number of properties in prime areas. She also acquired a piece of her own property in another area of Fajara we call Pipeline. She had the property built herself and rented it out. Mum got so hooked on construction work and on expanding the house that she ended up selling all the properties she inherited and used the funds to expand our house in Fajara, including a guest house located right next to our house that she decided she wanted to develop and manage herself. Before we knew what was happening, we were surrounded by neighbors in our own compound, with no more privacy and less space for us kids to run around.

It seemed as if we lived on a construction site. One friend, Modou Mboge, used to refer to our house as SOBEA whenever he came to visit my younger brother. SOBEA is an acronym for a famous French construction company that the government of The Gambia contracted on water and sewage assignments with the Gambia Utilities Cooperation. Dad would be gone for a week or two and Mum would have plumbers, electricians, masons, and carpenters in the house at the same time, knocking down walls and making changes and renovation works. It's a wonder none of my siblings and I caught up with asthma, tuberculosis or pneumonia growing up in that environment. When Dad arrived home from his travels and before he entered the house, Mum would blindfold him at the entrance of the living room, hold his hands and lead him to the spot where changes had been made in the house.

I do not think there is any part of that house that has not been knocked down. Both Mum and Dad enjoyed the renovation and changes, and once Dad saw the change Mum made, he would be inspired to propose another project or wall to extend yet another area in the house. Our family home has been reconstructed so many times, it is impossible to believe the "before" and "after" photos of our home over the years. My dad had demarcated our family home into three portions as well. As both Mum and Dad built, they were renting these properties. The rental income became useful for the university education of my siblings and me overseas.

Today, I can resonate why my mum, even after we have all left the nest, married with children, and with Dad now passed, refuses to move out of that huge house to stay in a smaller house. She built that house from the core and made it the home it is today.

In addition to the construction work in the house, Mum owned and managed a bookstore she named Chaakus Book-shop. I emerged from a fourth generation of affluent educated women. On her maternal side, Mum was related to the Addo, Lusack, Dixon Belle, Carayol, Jow, Evans, and Sowe (but pro-nounced Saww) families. However, the name of my mother's bookstore, Chaakus, is associated with my father's family name.

It is customary in some West African countries for one's surname or family name to be accompanied by a compound name. These are the family names associated at times either by a compound name or the name of one's ancestors. At special occasions, the *griots* (praise singers) use these names to identify an individual with a particular lineage. So Chaakus was the name associated with Dibba. We would then be referred to as Dibba Chaaku Wallimang, referring to the names of our great-great-grandparents. Similarly, the same exists for some Aku tribe household family names for example, «Lloyd Evans» or «Dixon Belle» although this is not as common as it is among the Wolof tribes.

My dad was born from a strong and influential clan on his maternal side. His mother, Oley Jack, hailed from the Jack, Cham, Gaye, Bittaye, Sillah, Jobe families of the gold and silver smith's clan. Historically, the *Wolof* tribes in the West Africa region were divided into occupational groups—the gold and silver smiths clan (referred to as *teega*), the praise singers or *griots* clan (referred to as *geuwel*), the clan responsible for man-ufacturing and designing leather (*oudey*) and so forth. During the ancient era, occupational groups had particular talents and skills to benefit the other. Intermarriage between the occupational classes was discouraged to maintain the talents, skills and knowledge of the ancestral lineages.

The clan of my dad's mother—the "Teega" Group—hailed goldsmiths, silversmiths and blacksmiths. They made the weapons used by the nobles going to war, jewelry, and farming tools. This clan was known to be multitalented, distinguished and educated.

My dad's father, Babou Dibba, on the other hand, hailed from the outskirts of the capital city of Banjul. He came from the provinces. His family origin was identified with the Mandingo tribe. Some family members have told me that one of our earlier ancestors was actually of Fulani origin, (surname Bah) from the Futa Jallon region. This great-great-grandfather migrated to The Gambia, where he was hosted by Mandingo families. When asked upon arrival in The Gambia in Mandingo what his surname was, which was customary practice, he explained to the interpreter at the time that his surname was Bah. As the interpreter passed on the message to the Gambian host he said "*affo di Bah*," meaning, "he said he hailed from the Bah." This I was made to understand was interpreted that the surname was Dibba and not Bah. I am unable to further verify the authenticity of that story, but either way, Mam Sally Dibba (one of my grand-aunts, sister to my paternal grandfather), and my sister Penda definitely resemble offspring from Fulani tribes.

Babou Dibba, my paternal grandfather, hails from Kani Kunda in Baddibu from the North Bank Region of The Gambia, and was brought to the city of Banjul by an affluent trader named Alhaji Babou Samba of the Sambene *griot* clan, a noble trader of his time. He brought my grandfather to Banjul as an apprentice and taught him the skills of sewing, and eventually arranged for his marriage. Given Alhaji Babou Samba's influence in The Gambia at the time, he was able to arrange for the marriage of Babou Dibba to Oley Jack, the daughter of an influential gold and silver smiths' family. This was an unusual union, as it was not common practice for the offspring of the gold and silver smith's clan to marry outside of their circles.

So both my father and *his* father married women from affluent families. My dad told me how strict and proud his father was, how he never wanted favors from anyone and how, as a tailor, was determined to do it all by himself to raise his nine children. My father and his eight siblings lived in a two-bedroom house and his dad ensured no one but himself provided for his family. He would not accept hand-outs from anyone.

I was told my grandfather seldom laughed. Allegedly he would often go to the market himself to get groceries for his family and he seldom allowed his wife to go visit her family on the other side of town. When my grandmother requested to visit her family, he would say "Okay, you can go, but make sure you are back in an hour or a couple of hours." Obviously, it would not make sense for my grandmother to bother going because by the time she arrived it would be time to return back to her matrimonial home.

As a young boy, before my grandfather had yet acquired a property of his own for his young family, my dad lived and partly grew up with his mum's extended family. He used to share stories about how when they lived in his mother's family compound, known as *Njaggen affdie*, he and his siblings were somewhat discriminated against by some of the members of the clan. Although their mother hails from that family, they were not 100% fully accepted as original and undiluted members of the clan. Perhaps it could be the reason why my father and two of his younger brothers opted to marry outside of the clan to their first wives. Or it may just have been a coincidence. It may also be the reason why some of his siblings were moti-vated and yearned to prosper academically and professionally in their lives. At least four out of the nine of them excelled academically and earned scholarships to pursue further studies outside of the country, thus acquiring excellent professional status in the United Kingdom and in The Gambia. One of my dad's brothers, an eloquent writer, was honoured with an

OBE (Order of the British Empire) by Her Majesty Queen Elizabeth II of the United Kingdom.

My father earned his status within the Gambian society and amongst his peers. He developed a selected circle of friends and became one of the founding fathers of the Rotary Club of Banjul. The year he was elected President of the Rotary Club, Miss World (1989) from Barbados paid an official visit to The Gambia and attended one of the Rotary Club's Annual Ladies nights. The wives of the Rotarians were called Inner Wheelers and my mum, naturally, was one of the members. My father had a beautiful home, a beautiful wife, four beautiful children and lived in a well-to-do neighborhood in a beautiful house. He had it all—academic, status, family, job, finances, etc.

When my parents travelled and returned home, it was a pleasure to watch us open up their suitcases and see the goodies they brought for us. My parents would return home with five to six suitcases of gifts, even for both my mum and dad's extended families. Mum hardly ever brought anything for herself. Everything she had or wore had to be bought by my father and always of the highest quality. Dad took pride in how Mum looked, and loved to be the one to buy her gifts like jewelry in gold and precious stones, clothes and accessories. And when he loved the style, he would buy three of the same style in different colours for Mum.

My parents entertained regularly at home and it was imperative that we were always well dressed and well behaved when visitors were in the house. My mum took it upon herself to teach us how to eat at the table, how to sit and behave at the table, how to interact with important visitors in the house.

As children, we had the best of everything at the time. We each had our own bedrooms, all well furnished and each room with its own air conditioner. When new music albums were released, we were the first to have them. Michael Jackson's Thriller was one such. When Michael had that red jacket with twenty-seven zippers on every part of the jacket, my parents bought an imitation version for my brother. We had the Jackson Five "Off the Wall" albums and other such records. And we owned the latest VCR cassettes of up-to-date Cosby Show, Different Strokes, Baby I'm Back—black comedy programmes from the USA. On Sundays, my dad played his favourite Jim Reeves records the whole day. He would sing along with the album whilst Mum would chorus on the other side of the house. They would also demonstrate to us how to dance the foxtrot. Years later, I was told by my husband that one of our friends who lived in our neighborhood growing up called us "the Cosby family" of Fajara.

We wore the best, ate the best and had the best growing up amongst most of our peers. As a Rotarian, Dad ensured we kids attended whenever the Rotary Club organised major events. My parents had us registered at the Fajara Club (then called Bathurst Club)—a prestigious membership club at the time for expatriates and upper/middle class Gambian families—for dance classes to learn Scottish Dancing, amongst others. We went to Marina International School, the most prestigious pre-school in The Gambia at the time. During those years, the school had a foreign head teacher and foreign teachers. The few Gambian children in the school hailed from upper class elitist families.

It was no wonder that my parents became troubled when I, their eldest daughter, somehow did not want to live up to the standards and expectations as the daughter of an upper class family.

AUNTY MAMA

As a little girl and then as a teen, I watched how obsessed and possessive my father was over my mum. Dad wanted to do everything together with her. They had to travel together, go out together and have the same friends. All of Mum's friends at the time were the wives of Dad's friends. Mum got married very early (at the time it was normal for girls to get married at a very early age) and had literally grown up interacting with no one outside of her family circle except those whom Dad introduced her to.

For as long as I can remember, my father travelled a lot all over the world. He would almost always take Mum with him. During their absence, my siblings and I would sometimes be under the care of my great-grand-aunt. She raised my mum and her siblings and also raised my maternal grandmother. Mum had three siblings from her maternal side. My great-grand-aunt was called Lucretia Ayeshemi St. Clair Joof. Mum and my youngest sister, Lu, were named after my great-grand-aunt. She raised so many other children under her care—nieces, and children of other relatives and friends, some of whom were widows, single, or could not afford to raise their own children—that as a result, many called her Aunty. My mum and her siblings called her Mama. As great-grandchildren growing up under her wing, we called her Aunty Mama.

Aunty Mama was tall, heavy built, and often wore Afro wigs. When I watch Big Mama movies or Madea's shows of

Tyler Perry, they remind me of her, except Aunty Mama was not aggressive and confrontational like Big Mama or Madea (well, not to us children at least, but perhaps my mum and aunts whom she raised and older people around her circles may not agree). However, she was the type who would go to battle for you if you needed it. If we got caught up in any neighborhood fights, she would march to the house of that child and demand that the child and parents come out and apologize.

I was not a fighter. In fact, I was more of a victim. Oftentimes the boys would take us to "Banana Island" behind the compound of my school and beat us up if we did not share our packed lunches with them. I would run straight to Aunty Mama's house after school whenever someone picked a fight and suggested we meet at "Banana Island" to settle it. One boy in particular was notorious for beating me up. He made it a point to kick me, or grab my bag and empty it out on the floor or take whatever food I bought outside of the school gates after school. He was a playground bully.

Once when I was still quite young and a student at Methodist Primary and Kindergarten School, I was talking with some of my classmates during lessons. The teacher tried to caution and stop us, but we went on talking every time she gave us her back and faced the chalkboard (we used to call it blackboard then). The teacher grabbed the duster she used to erase the chalk off the board. It was the size of a shoe brush with wood on all sides and one side with cloth. She threw the duster across the room and it struck my head. The classroom became still and so did I. I had a slight cut on my head, nothing serious. The bleeding dried up on the cut before the end of the school day and because I had cornrows on, it was difficult to see the cut unless one literally passed a comb through.

When I got home and told Aunty Mama, she marched to school with me the next day and went with me straight to the Headmistress's office. She demanded that the teacher be called. The teacher came to the Head's office and Aunty Mama went off on her. She demanded the teacher apologize to me and that she take me to the accident and emergency unit of the Royal Victoria Hospital. The cut did not even warrant a plaster. Perhaps a bit of surgical spirit to clean the area would have done the trick.

But Aunty Mama insisted so the teacher and I went to the hospital. They shaved the hair around the cut, cleaned it up, put some dressing on it, and we returned to school. I was so embarrassed I never told Aunty Mama about anything that happened to us in school again.

Thus that was Aunty Mama.

In hindsight, I believe, Aunty Mama sowed the seeds of empowering my mum. With no biological children of her own, she was a role model, mentor and mother to my mum, an anchor and pillar all in one. She made Mum how she turned out today—independent minded, confident, a visionary, a go-getter, someone who will not take any attack against her lying down. Mum used to explain how Aunty Mama would deliberately wait to go to church until after the service or mass had started. She would then majestically march slowly into church with her stiletto heels clicking on the floor as she found a spot in one of the front pews.

Aunty Mama was married twice to very influential lawyers, one of whom, named St. Clair Joof, was a well-known attorney and politician in his day. My siblings and I never met either of Aunty Mama's husbands. They died years before we were born. My mum told me stories about how Aunty Mama used to get involved, in an uninvited sort of way, in consultations between St. Clair Joof and his clients during legal consultations. She would offer unsolicited advice and counseling to the clients, to the amazement of both her husband and the client. Being married to influential husbands who were both lawyers, and one a politician, during the 1940s and 1950s seemed to have sparked her empowerment as an educated woman.

After the death of St. Clair Joof, Aunty Mama never re-married, but quite naturally engaged in politics. She became one of the most instrumental political women of her time in the People's Progressive Party (PPP) during the 1970s and was selected as the first female member of Parliament in The

Gambia. Growing up with Aunty Mama, we saw her come and go to political events. People were always at her house, she organised events, she had properties, she had influential friends, she travelled and as a widow she had a car and driver.

Aunty Mama lived on Perseverance Street in Banjul. In those days, the 1960s and 1970s, and perhaps even earlier, the design of one's house determined the status of the person. Her house was elevated on stilts, which gave the building a higher elevation, and was built like Creole houses in some Caribbean countries. In my *Aku* mother tongue, we would call it *tone ous*; which if translated into English should mean stone house, although it was similar to a storey building but not really one, as there was no first or second floor landing leading upstairs and downstairs. However, one would have to climb stairs to get into the house. At the time, houses were built with *rhun* palm sticks from the coconut palm tree trunks, called *kirintin* in the *Wolof* language, and then plastered with cement on the palm *rhun*.

Under the stilts, Aunty Mama bred ducks and chickens. She also had a hairy white household dog name Flush. I'm not sure where the name came from, but apparently she had a dog before with the same name, and when that one died she got another similar breed and gave it the same name.

Her kitchen sat outside on the back verandah of the house with a toilet and bath area next to it. There were no showers or bathtubs then. Instead we filled buckets with water from the tap outside. Then we would use a cup to pour the water to wash and rinse our bodies. Aunty Mama did have, however, a modern flush toilet, as we would call it. Most houses had pit latrines that were set up at the back of the compounds and were collected every evening or sometimes in the middle of the night by the city council latrine collectors. Because Aunty Mama's flush toilet was within the building, but still outside on the landing of the stairs, she had huge pans with lids that she would bring inside her bedroom in the evening in case we needed to use the bathroom at night. In the mornings, the pans would be taken outside, emptied, washed and left under the sun to dry until the next evening.

Aunty Mama also had an attic and as kids we were afraid of what was up there. Each time we were naughty, Aunty Mama would threaten to call upon the man with a white frock who lived up in the attic to come down and scare us. Although we never saw the man with the white frock—he was like the boogy man—Aunty Mama's threats always worked. We behaved out of intense fear of that strange man who lived in her attic and wore a white dress.

The adjoining room next to Aunty Mama's bedroom was called "the box room." It was like a walk-in closet where she stored her hats, suitcases of clothes, and shoes, as well as some of her valuable crockery and cutlery for when she was entertaining. When she would send us to the box room, we were always hesitant to go in there for fear of coming across the man with the white frock, given that the box room was also the entrance to the attic. All my life growing up in Aunty Mama's house, I never once went up into the attic.

Aunty Mama spoiled us as her great-grandchildren most of the time, but not always. She had her favorite chair positioned by the main entrance where she could watch everyone coming in and going out of her compound. As kids, when we wanted to sneak out into the streets to play in the neighbourhood, we would pass by the back and crawl on all fours as fast as we could to get to the gate. After she realised our plan, she hung a huge bell at the back of her gate. Not only did this make it heavy for us to pull the gate open but also, to make matters worse, the bell would ring with a loud dong. She would wait until the wee hours of the morning after we had returned home and were in the climax of our sleep. Then she'd storm into the bedroom, throw open the windows and whip us on top of the covers with her special cane that she reserved for such occasions. My cousins, young aunts and I (who slept together on the same bed when we were at Aunty Mama's) would scramble to hide underneath each other so the whip would hit the other person instead. There was nowhere we could run to hide. The doors were all locked and it was way too early to run outside anyway. Plus, we were so tired from playing and running around in the streets that all we wanted to do was go back to sleep. Aunty Mama knew how to get us to follow the house rules.

I cannot begin to count the number of times I got in trouble with my parents for going against the house rules at home, against the status quo. I was always the one to break the rules. Always. Not a month seemed to go by without me getting beaten, scolded, or punished for breaking house rules.

One day at home with my parents, we were at the family table having dinner. We each dished out the *cherreh* (millet grains simmered in hot water and served with lamb pepper soup) onto our plates and began to eat. I guess I may have dished out more on my plate than I should have, because when we all finished eating and I said I was full, Mum said I could not leave the table until my plate was empty. My siblings and dad left the table and Mum sat at the table with me to ensure I finished eating every grain. That was the longest dinner of my life.

Each time I tried to force a spoon into my mouth, I would want to throw up, spitting the food onto my plate. Still, Mum would tell me to pick up the food and put it back in my mouth. Choking, so full, I kept bringing up the food from my mouth and each time Mum would insist I grab the spoon and put it back in my mouth. I was crying, I was perspiring, I had snot coming from my nose. Every opening around my face had something coming out. After what seemed like forever, Mum must have also grown tired of sitting there and watching me force-feed myself. She got up, ordered me to clean the dining table and left me sitting alone. I emptied the plates, washed the dishes and went to bed. I hated *cherreh* from that day for a very long time. I neither wanted to see nor smell *cherreh* ever again. After that incident, I learned to take a little on my plate just in case I would get into trouble again.

Another time when I was around twelve, I decided to run the bath so my siblings and I could have a bubble bath. We watched the tub fill with bubbles and when it neared the top of the tub, Penda, Omey and I (Lu was more reserved and too young to join us) all jumped into the bathtub, causing the water to overflow out of the tub and out of the bathroom under the door. We had the bathroom door locked.

Mum must have seen the water gushing underneath the bathroom door. She banged on the door and demanded we open it. I climbed out of the bathtub, left my siblings inside, and attempted to open the door. With slimy soap on my hands I had a hard time turning the key to unlock the door. By the time I opened the door I saw the slippers in Mum's hand and I knew she was going to strike my wet soapy body. It had happened many times before: Mum's anger was at me because I was the eldest and should have known better.

I dived under her and ran towards the sitting room door. She chased after me. The sitting room door was unlocked and I dashed out, through the main gates and into the street. Stark naked with soapy bubbles clinging all over my body, I ran straight into a group of the neighborhood kids and others all stared with amazement. Some of the boys were three to four years older than me.

My mum stopped at the main gate when she saw the neighborhood boys walking past.

"Good evening, Aunty Lucretia," the boys said as they stopped to greet Mum. She smiled at them and responded to their greetings, and then turned around and walked back in the house. She left me standing naked, exposed, humiliated in the middle of the street.

By this time, my siblings had also left the bathroom and cleverly emptied the tub. We were just kids wanting to have fun, or so I had thought at the time. But I was the eldest. I should have known better. My mum walked to her room and shut the door on me as I returned to the mess with mops and a bucket. I had escaped the whipping this time, but the emotional trauma of being exposed and abandoned remained with me for a long, long time. What I felt was in sharp contrast to Aunty Mama's rescue from the schoolyard bullies.

In addition to the many nieces she raised, including my mum, Aunty Mama's generosity extended to other family members, friends and neighbors as well. Her house was equipped with a telephone, a radio, and a huge gramophone. There were no TVs at the time, but every month, she would arrange to have the government's film production unit come to the house and show us films through a projector of what life was like outside the confides of The Gambia. Neighbors, young and old, would come over for a couple of hours to see the United States, the UK, Israel and other countries as well as wildlife documentaries.

She hired contractors to build extra one- and two-bedroom quarters around the borders of her fence, which she rented out at very cheap rates to less fortunate families who typically came from the provincial areas. I admired her ease with which she gave so freely and shared with others who had less than she did, how she invited them into her life and embraced their hardships. I seemed to be drawn to her way of living, giving and sharing.

In spite of all the beatings, scolding and punishments I received at home, I still had the urge to break the house rules. From as early as the age of eight, I would sneak food from our kitchen and run outside in the streets to give them to our less fortunate neighbors, particularly those who were either drivers or watchmen working for our neighbors. I would steal money from my mum's purse and gave it to the poor when they came to beg for cooking salt or something relating to food. When I gave them the money I'd tell them my mum said to give you this so you can get extra food. I would take my own clothes and other personal effects and give them to my friends who I knew didn't have as much as I did.

There were times when my parents travelled that my mum's younger sister, Olive, and her husband came to Fajara to babysit us. I would insist to go and stay in Banjul with Aunty Mama instead. That was where my cousins and other young aunts lived and where the Methodist Primary and Kindergarten School was situated. The thought of being able to walk to school in the mornings with my cousins and young aunts, instead of always being driven to school by our family's chauffeur, excited me.

And I could buy my own lunch on the way to school instead of eating the lunch made by our house help and placed in a lunch box in my bag every day. At home I would often trade my packed lunch when I got to school or use it as a trade off from being bullied.

In Banjul I could buy tasty warm porridge being sold by Aunty Mama's neighbor at *Sabally Kunda* down the street. I could buy my lunch from the neighbor selling bread and *akara* (fried ground bean balls) wrapped in cement paper or pass by Aunty Maga to buy bread and liver in sauce. Sometimes I would save it for my school lunch, other times I'd eat it on the way to school.

I spent as much time as I could in Banjul. I looked forward to riding with my friends and cousins on the public transport, the GPTC (Gambia Public Transport Corporation) buses, back to Aunty Mama's after evening studies with Mr. Fowlis at Bakau School instead of going back home to Fajara with my siblings in our chauffeur-driven car. We would go to Grant Street to buy food from an elderly lady we called Aunty Ebeh. That was not her name, but the name of the dish she used to prepare and sell. *Ebeh* is a dish made of cassava and palm oil with assorted seafood, lime, pepper and seasoning. It was a popular dish that children enjoyed growing up and interestingly, to date, it is still a special dish for the younger generation, and some older ones too. My kids and I love it.

On one of my visits to Banjul, I went to the workshop of a goldsmith with my cousin Ida. I asked the goldsmith to remove the gold *karanyeh* earrings my parents had on my ears and put them on my cousin's ears because she didn't have earrings at the time. These were not the type of earrings that you could wear and take off every day. An expert goldsmith or silversmith needed to put them on and remove them with pliers.

When my parents found out what I did, they scolded me. But they could neither say much nor do anything to me because I had given the earrings to my first cousin whose father was my dad's elder brother. It was too sensitive for them to take any action, but I felt their disapproval just as strongly as if they had.

Aunty Mama was the best thing that happened in my life. My memories of spending time with her were the best memories I have as a child. There was no great-grandchild who did not have this affection with Aunty Mama and each of my siblings have their memorable stories to share about their experiences with her. Her influences rubbed off on my mum, and I believe, on my siblings and me as well, and ultimately on our children, particularly our daughters.

When she was in her mid 60s, Aunty Mama had a stroke and took ill. After Aunty Mama was discharged from the hospital my mum moved her to our house in Fajara. I moved into my younger sister Penda's room so Aunty Mama could occupy my bedroom, where sadly she died not long after on 16 August 1980, in my room and on my bed. I was thirteen years old at the time.

Our lives were never the same again.

BURNS AND SCARS

When I was fourteen years old I was preparing dinner one Sunday since it was my turn for the kitchen. I had oil on the frying pan as I was preparing French fries, which we would call chips at home. I lit the stove just as Lily, a friend of ours from the neighborhood, passed by to visit. After chatting for a few minutes, I decided to walk Lily home.

On my return, I found a billow of smoke in the kitchen and realised I had forgotten to switch off the stove. I rushed and switched it off, covered the oil-filled pan sitting on the stovetop, and left it to cool off. I returned to the kitchen a few minutes later to test whether the oil was cool enough to work with yet. I threw one thin slice of the fry (chip) into the oil and a burst of fire erupted in the pan. I grabbed a kitchen towel and held the handle of the frying pan, still with the fire blazing from that one chip in the pan. Just then, Omey, who was ten years old at the time, walked into the kitchen. I yelled at him to quickly open the kitchen door leading to the outside back yard so I could run out with the blazing pan. He ran to the door and held it as wide as he could as I ran outside with the pan.

The towel I used to hold onto the handle started to catch fire. I could feel the heat on my fingers as the fire penetrated through the cloth and flames engulfed the towel. I screamed, letting go of the pan. The hot oil splashed onto me as the pan clattered to the ground. Some of the oil reached my brother who was still standing by the doorway. He jumped as if he were climbing the wall.

I also jumped, and almost tumbled onto the tiled floor of the kitchen porch leading to the back yard, made slippery by the spilled oil. Fortunately, as one leg was about to go down, I stretched the other leg over onto the hard concrete floor away from the tiled area, and caught my balance rather than falling into the scalding oil. By this time, the fire from the pan had gone out, but the towel continued to burn until the breeze from the outside finally put it out. At least we saved the kitchen from burning.

My parents were inside and rushed to the kitchen when they heard the screaming and crashing of pans. My mum called out to one of our next-door neighbors who happened to be a nurse. She was like family to us. Her name was Sister Rebecca Njie but we called her Aunty Bilo. She rushed over and dressed my wounds on both my right hand and right leg. I suffered second-degree burns from the oil, and my little brother had minor burns.

It was not normal practice for us to go to the hospital unless one actually needed to be admitted into the hospital. The hospital actually came to us. We were surrounded by neighbors, four of whom were nurses and worked at the Royal Victoria hospital. We also had two medical doctors in our neighborhood. One of the medical doctors was a very close friend of my dad. He had his private practice. When we were not well, Mum and Dad would take us to this doctor friend for a medical consultation. His name was Dr. Sheriff Ceesay; we called him Uncle Sheriff. There was also a dentist who lived nearby. Going to the hospital was therefore reserved for a matter of life or death.

The evening I received my burns, there was a school concert at the Gambia High School. The concert title was "The Marriage of Anansi the Spider." The play emanated from a book on the tale of the Ashanti tribe of Ghana. We used the book about the Tale of Anansi in some of the schools' literature classes. At the time, there were only seven high schools in the whole of The Gambia, and the high school hosting the concert was a bi-product of a Methodist missionary school called Boys' High School, which my father had attended.

My parents did not allow me to go out in the evenings very often. It was one way they attempted to keep me under control. However, they had agreed I could attend the concert, particularly as it was a school-organised event. In our strict home environment, any opportunity to go out was a privilege. I was not going to let this opportunity slip by. After all, Aunty Bilo had already taken care of my wounds and she never said anything about not straining myself, or anything.

Nobody told me I should not cover the burns.

My burns were treated and the stinging had stopped so I put on a pair of long khaki-coloured corduroy pants and a long-sleeved cotton shirt to cover the sight of the burns. My siblings and I then went to the concert with the driver who dropped us off, waited for us until the concert was over and took us back home. Throughout the concert, I did not feel any pain. However, the hall in which the concert was being organised was hot. Ceiling fans rotated from the high ceilings, but had little effect. Most of the doors were closed except the main entrance hall and a couple of exit doors close to the stage. With several school children at the concert, the crowded hall was hot and sticky.

Outside the evening air was cool. Across the road from the school a slight cool breeze blew in from the Atlantic Ocean seaside, so one could feel the fresh air if one was brave enough to venture outside. I wasn't. The main Christian cemetery sat adjacent to Gambia High School, where the concert was being held. I was definitely not going outside of that hall close to the cemetery as a fourteen-year-old.

When we got home after the concert, I tried to take off the long pants and shirt. My skin from the burns followed the clothes as I removed them. I felt excruciating pain. I had peeled off the dead burned skin as a result of wearing long pants and sitting for three hours in an overcrowded, hot hall. My wounds became soggy with water oozing out of the different patches. I had about six large burn patches on my leg, three medium-sized burn patches on my hand, finger and my lower arm, and one huge one on my upper arm.

Aunty Bilo came by the next day to dress them, with strict instructions not to cover them up, to leave them open so the burns could dry up easily. Each day my burns got worse and infected to the point I could no longer walk; neither could I write as my fingers were also burned. I would not return to high school for a few months. I was confined to bed, with Aunty Bilo taking it upon herself to come over to our house every morning and evening to clean and dress my burns. I could not put on any clothes. I was partly covered with a light cotton sheet to protect the burns from flies and to avoid my accidentally rubbing the burns on anything around me.

Today, almost at fifty years of age as of this writing, I still have the scars to show. As a result, as a teen I seldom wore short clothes above my knee. I would either wear long pants, a long dress, a long skirt or our traditional outfit, which usually had a long wrapper. I was more comfortable with exposing the burns in my arms but not on my legs. It was not easy for a teenager to wear long clothing when mini was in fashion at the time. There were the rare times when I would brave it once in a while and wear a mini skirt. However, I would dust some make-up powder to cover the marks on my legs. At the time, "Fashion Fair" and "Island Beauty" were the make-up brands in vogue for us at home in The Gambia and I took the palettes with me everywhere I went. Over the years, as the burns healed, they left dark patches on my leg.

These dark scars represented the hidden, ever-growing scars that were developing in my young heart. I carried the humiliation of my parents beating me in the presence of my friends, causing my friends to tease me. I carried the humiliation of constantly being put down in the presence of my younger siblings. And I could not understand why. Why was I being punished for simply giving and sharing, for just wanting to be myself, something I felt so deeply I must do?

BREAKING THE RULES

When I told my parents I no longer wanted to go to Marina school, the private and prestigious school at the time, but that I wanted to go to a public school because that was the school some of my cousins attended, I think they did not make a fuss because it was, after all, a mission school and had its own status. It was the school that one was able to wear a uniform and I longed to be able to wear the same uniform as my classmates rather than the trendy clothes the privileged students wore at Marina school. My sister Penda would later join me at Methodist for a short while, but my father moved her back to Marina after the head teacher beat her up one day. I stayed on until it was time to move to high school.

I didn't know until many years later that my parents had considered sending me to Switzerland to attend a Ladette Finishing School for young girls so I would grow up to become a lady.

My parental restrictions and the many rules in the house most specifically set up for me, made me more and more rebellious. Naturally, my parents became disappointed because I was not meeting their expectations. The more rules, the more I rebelled, the more I got beaten and punished, the more I did what I did—hung out with my disapproved friends, gave away my clothes, shoes, bags, packed lunch, and jewelry. I knew what the consequences would be; that if my parents found out, I would be beaten or receive some punishment or another. I did not know or could not understand what continued to push me to do these things at the time, so I had to learn the hard way.

Being the eldest child in those days, and I presume perhaps to some extent to date, particularly as a girl in an African cultural setting, you were constantly in the spotlight, under the watchful eyes of your parents and everyone else who mattered in your life. In those days, it was every grown up's business to be in your business when you were a child, and every adult had a right to scold you if you did something you were not supposed to do, whether they were related to you or not.

At times some of us neighborhood kids would be standing outside in the street within our neighborhood and idling, especially around sunset. You could hear one parent yelling from inside their compound, calling all the kids to go indoors as it was getting dark. If it wasn't Aunty Bilo, it was my mum. Particularly those two. There was also Aunty Bertha on the other street. It was mostly the mums. The dads were usually quiet.

My siblings, particularly Penda and Lu, had friends who were mostly from other origins, children from distinguished British, Bangladeshi, Korean expatriate's families. Omey, as a boy, had mostly Gambian friends also. I felt more comfortable identifying with less fortunate friends and with relatives from my father's distant families. I was eager to share with them the beautiful gifts my parents brought for me from their travels overseas. Somehow, I always seemed to dig out friends from nearby towns in Serrekunda, Bakau or Banjul. Whenever I brought these new friends home, the first thing my parents would ask me was who their parents were. If they were not somewhere from my parents' circles, or from Fajara, they were not generally welcomed.

I did have some friends my parents approved of because they knew their families from our neighborhood in Fajara. With that group of friends, we would form clubs as young girls and refer to ourselves as "the Super Six" or "the Ebony Super Sisters." My friends Jackie, Annie, Asie, Amber, Cecilia, MA, Christine, Isha, Amie, Mama, Kinza and others would resonate with these stories; after all, the older boys and girls—mostly the older siblings of my friends in the neighborhood—also formed clubs like "Dramatics" for the older boys and "Funky Sisters" for the girls. As "Super Six" and "Ebony Sisters" we would organise club meetings, set up club rules—and perhaps most importantly—we would try to find ways of attending the older clubs' parties.

Many of the parties that I wanted to attend took place at night and most often did not come with invitations. They were usually put together by seniors—the "Dramatics" boys and "Funky Sisters" girls—and were announced by word of mouth. It was not a problem for my neighborhood friends to attend. They would ordinarily get permission to go; and besides, most of them had older siblings, some of whom were members of those clubs, so they could go with their older siblings. I didn't.

Going out to a party at night with no official, written invitation was a "no go" area for my parents.

Occasionally when I received a written invitation to a party in our neighborhood, or in the home of someone my parents knew and approved of, they would allow me to go, but insisted I take my younger sister Penda with me. As a teenager in high school, it just was not cool to go to parties with your younger sister. As well, Penda was not too keen on those kind of parties organised by local boys and girls in the neighborhood. She would go because of the conditions laid out on me. I soon realised also that she became my parents' informer and would often tattle on me.

Sometimes my friends would deliberately type an invitation letter for me to give to my parents. We would pretend the party was being held in the home of one of the friends whom my parents approved of, knowing their parents and all. Even with that, my dad would only at times agree, pending his mood, and demand I return home by 7pm or 8pm. This was the time when the parties were actually starting; sometimes the party didn't even start until after 8pm. Some parties started at 10pm or midnight.

So I would return home at the given curfew and wait until my parents went to bed and everyone was asleep. I would then creep out of bed, leave a pillow arranged on the bed to make it look like I was in bed under the covers and fast asleep, and head off to the party. A few times I got away with this trick. Other times I got caught into serious trouble.

First things first, my dad would bolt the doors so I could not come into the house. I would sit on the chairs in the patio outside and await my fate in the morning. This happened so often, I cannot count the number of times I had to sleep outside in the veranda or porch. Thankfully the parties were usually Friday or Saturday nights and mostly during school vacations.

One particular night my father refused for me to attend a special party. I was sixteen years old at the time. It was during the summer holidays, and a special twenty-first birthday of an older friend was being celebrated at the Causaurina Club, a walking distance from my house and near the beach. It was of was one of those parties that everyone in town was talking about. In fact, this party even came with proper invitations. And I got one through one of my friends.

Dad had travelled the week before and my siblings and I went with the driver to pick him up in Dakar, neighboring Senegal. It was a four- to five-hour drive. We had left home the day before, picked Dad up at the airport in Dakar and stayed at the Nina Hotel in Central Dakar. We bought lots of fruits in Dakar and then left early the next day to drive back to The Gambia. Dad was in a good mood and was excited to see us kids come pick him up together with the driver. So I thought this would be the best time to give him the invitation.

I handed Dad the invitation, a genuine one this time round. He read the invitation and then said no, I could not attend. I pleaded all the way from Dakar but Dad wouldn't budge. Everyone was going to be there; I would just have to brace myself for the consequences thereafter, but I was determined to go to that party.

The night of the party, I went to bed early. I had prepared my clothes and had everything ready and hidden. At around 11pm, when I thought everyone was in bed and fast asleep, I stepped quietly out of bed and got dressed. My party clothes included a white mini skirt with red trimmings ruffled around the skirt giving it double layers. I wore a red tube top with a jacket and had my legs dusted with Fashion Fair powder to cover the burn scars. I had long extension braids, a hairstyle I loved to wear during the holidays as we were not allowed to have them on in school. I walked across from our house to the party as it was not far from my house.

Obviously, my parents knew there was a party that night because I had shown them the genuine invitation. They knew exactly where and what time the party was being held. I was swirling my ruffles and having a fun time on the dance floor when someone tapped me on my shoulder. I was told my parents were outside and had come to pick me up. I knew that night was not going to be a good night.

I went outside and saw them. Both Mum and Dad were in the car, with Dad in the driving seat. As I slowly climbed into the backseat, I greeted them both but neither responded. My dad drove off. Given that the party was close by, it still seemed like forever before we arrived home. The stillness in the car felt heavy with tension.

When we got home, my dad grabbed me by the hand and led me to the study room that was behind their bedroom, to ensure my siblings could not hear him beating me, I thought. The fierceness in my dad's eyes warned me that this time was going to be different.

The beating was severe and long. After a time I could not even feel the belt cutting through me any longer. I got beaten so badly that my body went numb. I could no longer scream. I could not even cry anymore. When Dad realised I could no longer make a sound, and I figure he also got tired, he went into their bathroom. Completely dazed, I was flat out unable to see or hear anything.

My dad returned from the bathroom with a pair of scissors. He yanked my beautifully done long braids and with the scissors he chopped off all of the braids, cutting off my entire hair in the process. I was disoriented and did not realise what was going on. After Dad finished with me I left the study room, still dazed like a walking zombie. When I passed my mum I saw her look up at my head and start to cry.

I went back to my room and looked at myself in the mirror with my party clothes and make-up on. My hair was unevenly chopped off. Still too stunned and overcome to cry, I climbed into bed but could not sleep. Surely, I thought, Dad could not have tortured me so badly just because I defied his instructions and went to the party. No, really, there had to be more to it. He almost killed me, for God's sake.

The next day my mum and my siblings came to my room all in tears. Even my sister Penda, who always told on me, felt this one and she cried that day. I stayed in my room out of my father's sight for the rest of the weekend. Anyway, I was too sore to even move around. That afternoon, Penda brought some food for me in my room.

My mum offered to adjust the unevenness of my hair so it could look more shapely, and she trimmed it further down to a very low cut. After that haircut I decided to keep my hair short permanently. For a long time, until I left home for the United Kingdom for further studies, I kept my hair short.

The memories of that night haunted me until my fortieth birthday.

BIRD SET FREE

I had reached a point where I felt, that irrespective of what I did or did not do, no matter how much I tried to defend myself, whatever I said to my parents, they would not believe me. Sometimes even when my younger siblings did something wrong, I would be scolded for being the eldest and ought to have known better to stop them. Mum would beat me right along with the others for whatever they did. I felt like the scapegoat and the black sheep of the family, who would be picked on no matter what.

Yelling was what Mum did more of, particularly at me. What I resented most was when she would yell at me and make comparisons between my younger sister Penda and I in the presence of Penda.

Often, she would say, "Even though na you big, na you bigfull pass you lilly wan dem."

(Even though you are the eldest, you are more irresponsible than your younger siblings.)

"You lilly sister go take big na you hand."

(Your younger sister (and that was Penda) will be more matured and take on more responsibility over you.)

Those words felt like a knife being cut through my flesh. I preferred to have been beaten every day than to hear my mum say those things to me. It hurt so deep that I lost my morale, self-esteem and my confidence, which affected my academic performance. Dad, on the other hand, didn't talk much; neither did he beat my siblings. Only me. In fact, I am not sure I can recall ever seeing Dad beat up any of my siblings. My sister Penda on hearing these regular statements from my mum would take any opportunity therefore to tell on me and play the "good daughter" game.

The words and beatings haunted me for so long. Growing up, my friends made fun of me. Some would tease me and call me the "maid of my household." Even to date, some of my friends still express that I have come far in spite of what I went through growing up. They were at my house often and saw for themselves. My two other younger siblings, Omey and Lu, were not too involved in the struggle between my parents and myself, but they have been aware. My youngest sister Lu confronted Dad one day. She threatened him: "If you ever beat my sister again, I will kill you." I was not aware of that confrontation until Lu told me many years later. Penda, on the other, thrived on the fact that my parents always said she was the good one and I was the bad one. I guess because she was my immediate sibling, there would naturally be sibling rivalry.

I had bottled up the embarrassment, the anger and resentment at my parents, and at my younger sister Penda in particular, that my only consolation was to create an imaginary vision that I was not related to them. I started imagining that perhaps I was adopted and that was why I was different and was treated the way I was. I knew I was different; I didn't know how or why, but I realised that I was not drawn to the attractions of how they wanted me to be. I continued to be even more rebellious and more convinced that I did not belong to the family because they just did not understand me.

By some miracles, I left home to go to college in the United Kingdom in 1985 when I was seventeen years old. Being in the UK away from the control of my mum and dad after all those years was like the feeling of a bird set free by its captors. I started college in Watford and stayed in the women's hostel YWCA directly opposite my school, Cassio College, which made it easier to attend lectures. I studied catering and hotel management, my parents' career choice for me.

Having been taught to cook at a very early age, I actually enjoyed cooking and baking. It was no wonder some of my friends would tease me as the maid of the household. As a young teenager, I loved to cook and I was good at it. My parents probably assumed that because I loved to cook and bake, then catering was the right choice for me. They even had me registered at the Gambia Hotel School to get me all prepped for my catering career. I attended the Gambia Hotel School immediately after I finished High School. Yes, I loved to cook and bake, but that was as a hobby and not as a profession.

I had other plans.

I accepted to study catering and hotel management, more excited at the prospect of leaving home. My plan was never to return. Since I had been born in the UK while my father was a student at the university there, I was an official British citizen. I would not have problems living in the UK permanently.

I found a part-time evening and weekend job close to the college. During the day I went to classes and to work in a pizza restaurant in the evenings and weekends. To be fair to my parents, I did not have to work. My parents covered my tuition, accommodation, and pocket money for me going to college. Every teenager would have loved to not have to work, but again, this misunderstood young lady thought it was an exciting and different thing to do. It was my first time working. It also meant I had extra money of my own which I did not have to account for to my parents. I got the thrill from working—the thrill from being one with the other students who had to work to pay their fees, accommodation and stipend. I got the thrill from always wanting to be on the other side with those who did not have life on a silver platter. I got the thrill from turning my back against the status quo and everything that my parents wanted for me.

I believed they genuinely wanted the best for me, but on their own terms and conditions. I believed they wanted to provide for me the opportunity they never had from their parents. I believed they had their dreams and wanted me to live their dream, to fill the gaps in their life that they couldn't live when they were my age. That was what I thought. I felt they wanted me to be something I wasn't.

I appreciate that it is every parent's dream to have their child or children aspire higher than they did. I did not understand or appreciate what it was my parents were trying to give me until I had a child of my own and made the same mistake that my parents made on me.

A year before I left for the UK for studies, I had my first serious boyfriend, one I felt deserved being introduced to my parents. He was a lovely guy, honestly. Well mannered. Came from a good family. Of course my parents approved of him. They officially approved of my having a boyfriend I could bring home at the age of sixteen. He was allowed to visit me at home and even take me out on dates. He was the kind of guy that every parent dreams for their daughter—loving and caring and a real gentleman. He would often call me "my perfect sweet." His parents were equally welcoming and embraced me.

What did I do when I arrived in the UK? I left him. Why? I knew how my parents felt about him. They believed in him and trusted him.

This boyfriend was going for further studies to the USA and I was going to the UK. I left home a few months before he did. On his way to begin his studies, he passed by the UK and visited. We had a lovely time touring London together. When he left and headed off to college, I called off the relationship. A relationship my parents had given their blessings to. There I was, a young, immature woman trying to even scores with her parents. He did nothing to me. On the contrary. I called off the relationship just to get back at my parents for all the rage and hurt I'd experienced growing up. Due to the anger and the grudge I held against my parents, an innocent person was used in the crossfire between my parents and me.

But that was not enough. Not only did I call off the relationship, I married the first guy who asked me out, a coworker at the pizza restaurant. His name was Charles and he was from Nigeria. We dated for a few months and he proposed to me and without discussing or consulting with my parents, I accepted and got married at the registry in November 1987. That was a big blow not only for my mum and dad, but for my family. To crown it all, I did not tell them I was married or was getting married until they found out and asked me. At first I denied it, just to dig in the insult even deeper. I felt victory was mine and I got them where it hurt most.

In December 1988, Charles and I had a son. My parents by this time decided to accept that this was my fate even though they could not understand why I called off my relationship with the boy they approved of and got married so quickly to the first boy I met. They had no idea I was angry or that I was carrying so much grudge against them.

Charles and I rented a room in a shared accommodation on Chester Road in Watford. We were thus sharing the kitchen and bathroom with other tenants. Our reputation became tainted quickly as the other tenants overheard us fighting. When we learned I was expecting a baby we decided to get a mortgage and buy a property outside of Watford. We did not want to raise our child in a house in which we shared quarters with other tenants. Besides, we were thinking the change of environment would improve our relationship.

We bought a two-bedroom semi-detached in Aries Court in Leighton Buzzard in Bedfordshire. It was difficult for me to get a job there. I finally found a part-time job working in the neighborhood Circle K as a store assistant. Charles would only allow me to go to work when the store opened at 6am until mid-day when he would wake up and get ready to drive to work. He worked as store manager for Pizza Hut on Edge-ware Road all the way in London and would drive to and fro every day to work, leaving around mid-day and returning after midnight when the restaurant closed.

Because I had already started my prenatal care in Watford, I continued to go there and ultimately, our son was born on 19 December 1988 at Watford General Hospital. When I went into labor, Charles was at work so I had to call an ambulance. My dad was in town in London at the time and I called him to tell him that I was in labor and was heading to Watford

General Hospital. By the time Charles got to the hospital, I had already given birth. My dad was actually the first at the hospital and the first to carry my son even before Charles and I did.

I was typically at home on my own with Junior during the day until Charles returned home from work around midnight. In the morning I would leave for work at Circle K. Charles would stay at home with Junior until I got off work at noon. As soon as I got home, he would leave for work. This was our routine.

Junior did not have a life except with me at home and we realised this was not good for his growth and development. To cut the boredom, I would occasionally have Charles drop Junior and me off at a friend's, the Joshua family's house in Watford, on his way to work. They were from Nigeria so it was easy to communicate with them. Junior and I would stay and visit all day and into the evening until Charles passed by and picked us up after midnight.

We decided to find a babysitter who watched children in her home within the neighborhood so Junior could interact with other children. We found Linda, who fell in love with Junior the first time she saw him, and so did Linda's children, Louisa and Gary, and her husband Graham. They lived on Pegasus Road, walking distance from our house. Linda would come to be a great pillar of support to Junior and me.

My marriage with Charles did not last long. He drank a lot. He would go through a whole bottle of Remy Martin Brandy every single night when he got home from work and I became his punching bag for whatever reason. He would smoke a full large packet of Dunhill International cigarettes a day. As time went on, Charles was coming home later and later. Sometimes, he would call and say he was sleeping in the restaurant because it was very busy that night and that he was too tired to drive all the way to Leighton Buzzard. Understandably. Turns out he was involved with another girl who worked in the restaurant.

Charles and I fought almost every night, often getting the police involved. Every time the neighbors heard my screaming and Junior crying, they would call the police. The police would turn up and Charles would explain to them that it was just a domestic issue with his wife, and they'd leave. It got to a point whereby our house was constantly under police watch. Sometimes, the police would drive by just to see if there were any incidents. We were a minority in the neighborhood so it was understandable that we stood out. There were not many blacks living in Leighton Buzzard at the time. Actually, I only knew of one Jamaican lady, Maria, who was married to a white guy. Otherwise, it was pretty much only our little family.

A few times when we had a fight, the police insisted on seeing me rather than just speaking to Charles at the front door. He would usually not allow them inside the house. I would be upstairs clutched to Junior, both of us crying. When I had the courage to be bold and come downstairs, the police took Junior and me to the police station to keep us safe out of Charles's reach as he was fully under the influence of alcohol. They advised me that they could not do anything about the domestic violence unless I filed an official complaint and pressed charges, but I didn't understand what the implications of pressing charges were. So I never did.

I also was too ashamed to tell my parents. They had no idea how angry and bitter I was. The entire battle of scoring points with my parents had been in my head alone. Now, the thought of having to go back to them for help after a failed first marriage, made me face all the reality of what I'd done. Had I listened to them and done things the way they wanted me to, I would not have been in this mess. Had I accepted to be the kind of daughter that they had envisioned, things would have been different. The fear of them saying to me "We knew this was going to happen. We knew you would mess up and that you would fail" kept lingering in my thoughts. Mum was right, I was not going to make it and this was enough evidence.

But I could not swallow my pride and cry for help. Dying was an easier escape route than facing my parents and hearing my mum repeat the words that "I was not going to make it in life."

I attempted suicide. Twice.

The first time, Charles was around. He realised I was not

getting up that morning for work and found me lying on the bed lifeless. He called for an ambulance. I was rushed to Luton General Hospital, where I was admitted and my insides flushed of the overdose of painkillers. A very painful experience. Naturally, before I was discharged, the doctors needed to file a report and they asked me what happened. I explained. They double-checked with the Police Station in Leighton Buzzard who confirmed that they were aware of our domestic situation, but that I was not keen to press charges. The hospital filed the report.

Because our babysitter Linda and her family loved our son, she would drive over in the morning and pick up Charles junior for the day without charging us, even on days when we hadn't schedule her to babysit. I was terrified to leave the house. Charles senior would not allow me to go out.

The second time I tried to commit suicide, a few months later, Charles was at work and Junior was with Linda. I had given Linda a set of extra keys to the house in the event of an emergency. Linda returned to drop off Junior and rang the bell several times and I did not respond. She took the keys, went through the back gate and through the kitchen door, and rushed upstairs. She knew I had not gone out because I would not dare go out without Charles, even to Linda's house. When she discovered me unconscious, she called for an ambulance. They took me to the same hospital and went through the same routine. This time, the doctor warned me that I could end up losing my son to welfare if this practice reoccurred. It was a wake-up call for me.

The next time my husband beat me, it was so bad he threw me from the top of the stairs. I tumbled all the way down to the bottom stair, with my head hitting against the railings during the fall. I blacked out and I'm not sure how long I was out. When I recovered, I could see my son standing at the top of the stairs screaming "Mummy!!" He was almost turning two, but was afraid to crawl down the stairs.

I looked around to find Charles, who was by now sprawled on the couch passed out. I crawled up the stairs, grabbed my son, and tiptoed past the living room where Charles was snoring on the couch. When I reached the kitchen back door, I opened it as quietly as possible and ran to Linda's house. I had no shoes on. We lived next to the park so the grass, although soft, was wet. I was too scared to feel the autumn cold. I was more concerned about my son whom I hugged so tightly, I could not even hear him breathe.

It was after midnight when I rang Linda's doorbell, not stopping until all the lights were turned on in their household. I woke them all up. Linda and Graham had now had enough. They demanded I stay the night and insisted I file for charges.

Linda and I went to the house the next day to get some fresh clothes for Junior and myself. We waited until we knew Charles had gone to work. I had not even realised that our next-door neighbors had their house up for sale until I saw the "for sale" sign that day. They had probably gotten fed up with us. Our neighbors were a young white couple. I don't know if it was because of us or not, but they sold their property and moved away.

I could have broken my neck or my back being pushed down those stairs. I wanted to die anyway; I had made two attempts already. I was tired—emotionally, psychologically and mentally. The realisation that this relationship was traumatizing my son was in itself enough motivation for me to press charges. How much has my baby seen? How much does my baby understand about what was going on? Was he aware of what was happening? I didn't know. All I knew was that I saw his excitement whenever he was around Linda and her family.

I could not understand why, and how, I was always drawing attention to so much drama in my life. Enough was enough. It was time I filed charges against Charles and I summed up the courage with Linda's support and encouragement. I was initially reluctant because it would have meant returning back home to The Gambia a failure. By this time, my parents had become very supportive, but they were not aware of what was happening in my life. They visited Charles and me twice, during which time, Charles was on his best behavior. He also felt resentment that my parents did not approve of him. It was not that they did not approve of Charles, they did not approve of the way we got married without consulting them. Whenever my parents visited, my mum would bring lots of gifts and money for Junior and me. In fact, when I got pregnant, before Junior was born, they paid for me to visit (together with my siblings) them in the Seychelles on vacation. I believe it was their way of assuring me that I was still their daughter. In hindsight, I think my parents may have sensed that things were not working out in my marriage with Charles, but they never asked me and I do not think if they had, I would have said anything. Even as I was pregnant, I had lost so much weight. Whilst we were in Seychelles, Mum tried to raise the discussion a few times, but I brushed it off and pretended all was well. What I know now is that as a mother, you have that special gift to feel your child's pain, and I believe Mum did.

In the Seychelles, I felt even more uncomfortable. I did not feel I fit in the family anymore. I felt like a complete stranger and somehow withdrew emotionally. My parents tried to make me feel comfortable and we enjoyed the sightseeing and shopping as I pretended everything was okay.

I was too embarrassed to let them know. Only Linda and the Joshua family were aware. I would usually confide to Yetunde, the wife, but they were too far away in Watford to do much.

And yet I was determined not to be a statistic: a young African abused single mother, unemployed, commonly on suicide watch. I decided to seek legal aid and file a court order against Charles, as well as for a divorce, at the Milton Keynes County Court. I went to court and got the police, the neighbors, and the hospital to testify. There were enough records and witnesses. During the divorce proceedings, the court placed an injunction against Charles not to come within 100 metres around Junior and myself. He was asked to leave the property.

Charles stopped paying the mortgage. We were now three months in default of the mortgage repayment. Bills and letters started piling in. Then someone close within Charles' family called me to tell me she overheard that Charles, his sister, and brother were discussing taking Junior to Nigeria. Their mother wanted her grandson to come and live in Lagos with her. According to my informant, the plan was for Charles's younger sister to come to my house and request to take Junior out for the day. Once she had him away from me she would take him to Nigeria. What I hadn't realised was that Charles senior had taken Charles junior's original birth certificate and had applied for a passport for him.

As soon as I got off the phone with the news of my son's potential kidnapping, I called Linda. She advised that I inform my lawyer and immigration authorities, but I was too emotional, scared and confused to take action. I sat on Linda's living room floor, clutched to Junior, listening to her frantically making calls to the local police, my lawyer, and others with enquiries on my behalf.

Everything became blurred to me. The only thoughts going through my mind were *How could all these things be happening to me? Why me? Was it because I challenged my parents and was now reaping the implications of disrespecting my parents' authority?* The answers could not come through. All I felt was a force inside my head that it was time to return to The Gambia. Shame and guilty or not, I had to return home. *But home to where?* My parents were in the Seychelles where Dad was working as the Managing Director for the State Assurance Corporation of Seychelles; our house in Fajara was rented out; none of my siblings were any longer in The Gambia. Aunty Mama was dead. The only people I was close enough to go home to was my mum's sister Olive and her family. At that point, I decided, that yes, I would go and stay with Olive. Mum and Dad were planning to return home later that year anyway so a few months staying with Olive and her family while I waited for Mum and Dad might be good.

Linda drove me to Milton Keynes County Court for the first hearing for our case. Charles senior never appeared. There were three hearings and he didn't show up for any of them. He was subpoenaed and still they could not find him anywhere.

What I hadn't known was that apparently he did not have

legal status to stay in the UK. After his studies in the UK, he did not sort out his residential status to remain in the UK and was banking on me to apply for his status to remain in the UK on marriage grounds. I started to panic when we did not know his whereabouts. We were constantly in fear of Charles and his family abducting Junior. We instructed all immigration ports, from Dover to all airports around the Luton and London areas, about Charles and his family's plan to abduct my son and take him to Nigeria.

When the bank sent its final letter to repossess the property, I moved out of our house and stayed with Linda and her family as the case continued on.

I eventually swallowed my pride and contacted my dad's brother, but I was still too ashamed to call upon my parents. My uncle was then residing in the UK. I explained to him what was going on and gave him permission to alert my parents. When he contacted my parents Dad requested that I return home to The Gambia. He was sending money to my uncle to purchase a ticket for Junior and me.

The court by this time had granted me "Decree Nisi." We had to go through the final process for me to have "Decree Absolute," which would formally annul the marriage contract with Charles in absentia. The day before I was due to travel to The Gambia, I went to court for the final time and signed my divorce certificate, but I couldn't take it with me because the certificate still required additional administrative processes to record the judgment. In the absence of a divorce certificate, I could not remarry. Secondly, in the Muslim religion, it is not accepted for a Muslim woman to marry a Christian man, but it is okay for a Muslim man to marry a Christian woman. I needed the certificate to keep my options open for possibly remarrying in the future. My lawyer promised that they would send the divorce certificate to my uncle in Bletchingly in Surrey who would later mail it to me in The Gambia.

After a short-lived marriage that lasted only three years and four months, I left the UK in March 1991 with nothing but my son and one suitcase of personal effects. Everything else was left behind. Part of my belongings remained at Linda's and the rest was trapped at the house, which the bank had already repossessed. I returned to The Gambia ashamed and disappointed with myself, having to start my life all over again with my son now two years and three months old.

I had been keeping a diary of the entire marriage and relationship with Charles so that in the event Junior asked me about why I separated from his dad, and I may be too emotional to explain, he would be able to read it for himself. I kept the diary with the intension of giving it to him when he was old enough to understand. I felt if he had the diary, he could share it with his dad if the opportunity ever arose for them to meet. I realised there were two sides to every story, and that the diary was my side of the story with what were perhaps my own issues, and perhaps his father could one day give him his own perspective and his side of the story.

When Junior was a young man, he came to stay with my second husband and me in Nairobi, where we were living at the time. I called him into our bedroom and showed him the diary. It had a black hard cover with red binding. I explained that everything he needed to know about the first two years of his life was in that diary. He took the diary from my hands and listened to me. Finally, he said he did not want to know what was in the diary and that as far as he was concerned, Bye Malleh Wadda (my current husband, who adopted him when we got married and changed his name), was his father. I was disappointed when he destroyed the book. (Junior confessed to me many years later that he had in fact come across the book when he was around ten years old and had read it. At the time, a lot of things did not make sense to him, but what caught his attention was the incident when I was pushed down the stairs. He is still haunted by that.)

As Junior was growing up we never talked about it. He never asked me, not even to see a photo of his dad or what he looked like. I tried to show him a photo of Charles, but he tore it. We had attempted to contact Charles when Junior was around eight years old. My husband, Bye Malleh, was travelling to

Sweden with Junior for holidays. He wanted to adopt Junior and desired Charles's blessing (out of courtesy) to proceed. He also wanted to give Junior the opportunity to meet his father.

I searched for Charles's contact details and when I got them, I gave them to Byes. He planned to contact Charles upon their arrival in the UK where they were transiting through to Sweden. Byes managed to contact Charles on the phone and he agreed to meet at a particular location. Unfortunately, Charles never showed up.

We lost contact with him thereafter.

Upon Byes' and Junior's return from Sweden, my sister Penda, who is a lawyer, went through the process of filing the adoption process and change of name. The judge at the time was Patricia MaCcauley from Sierra Leone. Junior's name was changed from Charles Etuk Emmanuel Udom to Omar (after my father) Malleh (after Byes himself) Wadda. My father-in-law conducted Junior's conversion from a baptized Christian to a Muslim. I watched the conversion process as my father-in-law whispered and recited words into my son's ears and asked him to repeat selected prayers and affirmations after him.

I am not sure if Junior fully understood what was going on. He was excited and fascinated that he was going to have my dad's name and Byes' name and that he would share the same surname as all of us, including his younger sister Katty who was by this time already born. The part he did not enjoy in the process was when my father-in-law shaved off his hair with a razor commemorating that he was a newborn Muslim. My oldest son is now officially called Omar Malleh Wadda.

EXPECTED OF A WIFE

Not long after I returned back home to The Gambia, I met my second husband. We have been married for more than twenty-three years now. The first time my future husband and I met was while I was staying at my aunty Olive's house with her family, just a few months after I returned from the UK with Junior. An old friend came to visit. He brought another friend with him and they stayed for supper. After our mutual friend introduced us and they left, I didn't see my future husband again for about six months.

When I met my future husband again, I was working as a personal assistant to the financial controller in one of the five star hotels in The Gambia, a benefit of my degree from Cassio College in Watford in catering and hotel management. I did not recognize Byes, although he argues that I did and was pretending not to.

My boss, who was secretary of the board, had asked me to gather some documents for her to discuss at the board meeting, which she was currently attending in a nearby office. While I sat in the secretariat preparing the papers, a man who was also attending the board meeting as representative for his organization kept entering and leaving the meeting room. He appeared to be looking for excuses to walk into the secretariat. He requested to use the phone; another time he came out of the boardroom to ask for something else.

Finally, I remembered him when he introduced himself

and reminded me that we had met when he accompanied our mutual friend to my aunt's house for dinner. Thinking nothing of it, I kept wondering to myself how he could be making a meaningful contribution during this meeting if he kept going in and out of the meeting. Either way, I took it upon myself to mind my own business and let him figure out what it was he was trying to look for.

A couple of months later, he came to our office to see my boss. There was already somebody with my boss in her office so I asked him to wait. As he waited, he became very chatty and kept going on about some property he needed to go sort out. Eventually my boss came out from her office and motioned for her visitor to come in. As he walked into my boss's office, he turned around and said, "We need to finish off this conversation over dinner."

"If that dinner ever happens, I will pay for mine," I replied.

After his meeting with my boss, he left.

A few days later, he called me at home. When I answered the call, I asked him how he got my home phone number. He responded, "That's for me to know and you to find out." He said he was calling about the dinner date. I explained that I had to check in with my dad first to ascertain if it was okay. My parents had returned from Seychelles so I was once again living under their roof. I was now twenty-four years old with a son, but I still had to ask Dad for permission to go out. For Dad, as long as you were living under his roof there were certain rules and conditions everyone in the house had to adhere to. And needing his permission to go out, for reasons other than work, was still one of them. I asked Dad and he agreed. We set a date for that weekend.

On the evening of the date, my future husband, Bye Malleh Wadda, came in and met my parents for the first time. That evening we went out for dinner at a restaurant not far from my house. After we'd eaten, we were about to leave when a gentleman came up to us. He had been drinking. He said to my date, "Let me see the palm of your hand."

After looking closely at Byes' hand, he asked to see mine.

Puzzled, I held my palm out to him. Then he said, "You two are going to get married. Mark my words. My name is Hydara and I am a *sheriff*." *Sheriff* is a name given to a particular religious sect in the West African region; they are claimed to be descendants of religious gurus. "When I say something is going to happen," he said, "it will happen."

Not knowing quite what to think, I tried to not take the man seriously. I had just come out of an unhappy marriage and did not want to get myself meddled up again. After Hydara left us, we decided to walk back to my house. It was a lovely cool December evening, so upon reaching our street junction, we decided to continue on and strolled down the Fajara beach. Byes started telling me about himself, who he was and what he does.

I was being very cautious.

He said he was looking for someone with whom he can have a steady relationship. He said, and I quote, "I want someone to love, and to be loved." Our kids often laugh at us now when we explain to them how we met and what their dad said, especially this statement.

After only a couple of weeks into the courtship, Bye Malleh Wadda said he wanted to marry me. I thought it was way too early to start talking about marriage again for me, and even for us. We hardly knew each other. I told my mum about it and she mentioned it to my dad. My dad, being who he was, enquired through my uncles to find out more about Byes. The feedback was not positive.

My dad was told that Byes was not a serious person, he loved to party and that in fact he was already seeing someone else. I was not aware he was in another relationship. When my dad shared with me what he had heard, he confided that he did not want me getting hurt twice. He urged that he did not think Byes was the right person for me, that I was still vulnerable and may get hurt again. When the news about our courtship spread, several people cautioned my dad and my uncles that I should not marry this man.

In the meantime, Byes told his parents of his intension to

marry me. On that side, also, there was a problem. His mum wanted him to marry the girl he was seeing prior to me. He told his mum he was no longer seeing that girl and that I was the one he wanted to marry. To add another complication, some members of his family argued that he could not marry me because my father came from the *taiga* gold and silver smith's clan. Tradition does not allow anyone from their family to marry into a *taiga* family.

This time my family felt insulted. The marriage was not going to happen. They would arrange for me to marry someone internally from the clan. My dad called off the relationship and told Byes not to see me anymore.

Byes tried to call and I would not answer. He drove to the gate of my house and requested the watchman to tell me that he was outside. I sent a message back that I could not see him anymore. This went on for months. Each time he made attempts to meet it would fail.

After his continued persistence for several months, I finally agreed to see him again, against my dad's wishes. Every evening, we would sneak and walk down the beach, sit and watch the sunset. We found a favorite meeting point on the beach and would just sit and talk as we watched the sunset. We would talk about the different rumors going around both sides of our families. There wasn't much we could do.

Then one evening Byes informed me he had given his parents an ultimatum. He was in his early thirties and under a lot of pressure from his family to get married and settle down. He accused that now that he had found the woman he wanted to marry and settle down with, all sorts of excuses started coming out. He told his parents that if he were not allowed to marry me, then he would return to the United States (where he had lived and studied) and marry a foreigner and not return home.

One evening my dad called me to the living room, where I found him sitting with three of my uncles, all with stern faces. One of Byes' uncles had been to see him my dad, stating that my husband would like to ask for my hand in marriage.

My dad and uncles asked me whether I was still interested in marrying him. I was quiet. It felt uncomfortable answering this awkward question to these grown up men who had long opposed the marriage. After what seemed like a long pause, I said yes, that I was interested in marrying him.

It turns out Byes was able to win the hearts of some of his family members. His uncle from his mother's side took it upon himself to speak to my father. He was able to convince my father that Byes was a good young man with a kind heart and that he was in love and really wanted to marry me.

We dated two years before we got married. This time I had a real Gambian wedding.

The process for the traditional wedding began. The bride and groom are not involved in the consultation regarding the traditional process between the two families. The only time I was ever involved was when my uncle, Uncle Charles Jow, who was delegated by my dad to take the role as father on my dad's behalf (which is customary in our culture) asked me the date of my last menstrual period to make sure that the date of my wedding night did not coincide with my cycle.

We got married on 3 December 1993, two years to the day of our first date and the strange encounter with the Sheriff who had read our palms. Our wedding was an entire weeklong traditional ceremony.

As in traditional weddings of this nature, male and female relatives of the bride and groom are assigned to different roles. Seeking a hand in marriage, negotiation of the bride price or dowry, and the actual officiating of the marriage itself is negotiated by the male members of both families. The bride and groom are not actually present during this process of ne-gotiation amongst the men. The women's roles are typically assigned to the preparation process for the actual ceremony, the music and dancing and the exchange of wedding gifts from the groom to the bride (which is called *Meaye bu njaikah* in *Wolof*—the bride's first gift from her husband to be). The only time in which the men and women come together during a wedding ceremony of this nature is if there is a formal reception and during the evening time when the bride is being advised about her role as a wife prior to being handed over to her husband on the night of the wedding.

On our wedding day, after having my hair and makeup done by Vicky, I spent the day at my aunt's house (from my mum's side). The religious part of the ceremony was concluded by the men in the mosque around 5pm. In the evening I changed into my bridal dress and proceeded to my parent's house. Our entire neighborhood was filled with cars and people. The drumming and dancing had to be done outside in the street because there wasn't enough room in the compound to fit all of the guests. Following tradition, my many sisters-in-law came to con-gratulate the bride. Then drumming started and my in-laws gave me money for me to present to the drummers and to the *griots* who were singing praises about the bride's and groom's families. This went on until night.

I was then taken indoors to my parent's bedroom where all of my aunts and mum were waiting. An old woman gave me a bath—a tradition in which the bride sits naked on a mortar and is bathed with herbs and some prayers recited. After being changed into a loose, casual, traditional white cotton outfit with my head covered, I had to crawl three times in and out under my mum's legs. Then one of my sisters-in-law led me out of the house and around the neighborhood as other sisters-in-law and female elders followed us chanting.

Thereafter, they brought me back to the compound for the millet ritual, in which they covered my head and then mea-sured grains on my hands onto a basket. They sat me down on a mat outside where the men and women were all gathered to share advice about the dos and don'ts of marriage and what is expected of a wife towards her husband and her in-laws.

In the meantime, Byes and his friends were waiting in a room inside my parents' house for the bride to be officially handed over to them. After what seemed like forever of long speeches, I was lifted from the ground and led to where my husband was waiting. I had to crawl on all fours into the room to the foot of the bed where my husband and his friends sat, as did my cousin, Fatim, who was my bridesmaid. My husband lifted me up on the bed. His best man did the same with my bridesmaid.

With all of us sitting, one of my cousins carried a calabash of porridge and sour milk and placed it on the bed. The myth dictates that if the husband places his hands inside the calabash first then the first child of the couple would be a girl. If the bride's hand is first, the first child would be a boy. As soon as the calabash was placed on the bed, my husband's sisters and cousins tried to hold my hand so he could put his hands in first. At the same time, my cousins were trying to hold my husband's hands so I could put my hands in first. I am not sure who did first. By this time, I was overwhelmed and tired. The bed that had been prepared with white sheets for us to sleep on ended up being covered in porridge and sour cream in the struggle.

When that was all over, everyone left the room and left the couple to sleep. How can anyone sleep after all that drama, one would wonder? This process is called *jaebaleh* (meaning you are finally being given to your husband).

After everyone had departed and we were alone, my new husband told me he was travelling to watch a football match in Sierra Leone with his friends the next day. It was the first I heard about his plans and I was shocked. I could not convince him otherwise. I cannot describe how much I cried that night on my wedding night. It was as if my husband was a stranger. I cried the whole night. In the morning when Byes consulted with his friends they advised him that it would be best that he does not travel, so he cancelled the trip and his friends went without him.

The following day other traditional symbolic processes continued, like washing some of my husband's clothes and pounding millet (with a pestle on a mortar), with support from my sisters and cousins as well as from my sisters-in-law. Again, singing, drumming and dancing as this process goes on. These traditional symbolic processes only involve the women. This process is called *bulufelleh* and demonstrates the role a wife must play in her new home to her husband.

Then there was the night of *teg asset*. The female members of both sides of the family, as well as their friends and supporters, meet to give away money—dishing it out until early hours of the morning—to acknowledge and recognize the *griot,* the cousins, all those who prepared the dishes during the entire wedding process. *Teg asset* means putting money on a plate to give to those who have rendered services during the wedding ceremony.

Finally came the day I was taken to my husband's house. My sisters-in-laws came to pick me up from parents' house. My mum spilled some water on the ground and prayed for me. I hugged my mum, walked over the water and followed my in-laws—not allowed to look back. I could hear my mum crying. The reality that I will not be allowed to visit my mum for a period of time after I have left my family home to join my husband was painful enough. I cried until I arrived at my husband's house where my mother-in-law and other women of my husband's family welcomed me as a new member of their family.

On the seventh day my aunts brought all the gifts our family and friends had given me for my wedding. These included the utensils, crockery, pots and pans my mum had started buying and collecting in preparation for this day. A truckload of gifts and my personal effects were brought, which marked the end of my traditional wedding ceremony.

Many people in The Gambia who knew both my husband and me were not convinced our marriage would last. Some of his friends placed bets that it would not last two years.

ABANDONED IN MARRIAGE

Like most young women married in those days, especially for those of us who read *Mills and Boons* novels, my expectation on marriage—even second time around—was more of a fairy tale. I came into the marriage all excited to please my husband, to make him happy, covering up my own feelings; expecting that my happiness was determined by how happy I made him. I also had expectations that my husband was to be the head of the household.

However, my husband wanted to continue living just as he was: a bachelor. His understanding apparently was that he was expected to marry a wife, bring her home, provide for her, pay the bills and that was it. It really had not dawned on him that his life needed to change. Unfortunately, my husband did not get advice on how to be the head of the household or how best to engage with his wife. Traditionally within the African contexts, women were groomed in preparation of their expectations as a wife, mother, running the home and pleasing their husbands and his family; but most particularly, how to exercise patience against all odds in your marriage and relationship with and towards your husband.

After my first brief marriage, I remarried so I did not have to remain under my parent's watch, especially under the severe hand of my father. In the beginning I saw the marriage as an opportunity to regain the independence I had found in the

UK, lost, and found again. The excitement of freedom of not having to live with my parents again thrilled me. I had dreams of what I expected my marriage to be.

When I realised that this was not the reality, I became disappointed. Byes and I had been raised differently and I knew that naturally there would be some adjustments required, mostly from my side. I was raised in a strict and controlled environment. My family had been warned that my husband was irresponsible.

Bye Malleh Wadda was a thirty-something-year old, care-free, young man with no worries in the world. He loved to have a good time. Wherever there were parties, barbeques, and guys milling about, that was where one would find my husband and where he wanted to be. Other times, my husband would invite his friends over to our house for a barbeque or just to hang out until late at night or sometimes early hours of the morning. Occasionally some of his friends would come knocking at our doors and windows at 2 or 3am to hang out.

Come to think of it, is that not the freedom I wanted as a teenager? Was that not some of the main reason I challenged my parents?

Byes and I were living in Kotu about fifteen to twenty minutes from my parents. He had built the house in preparation for my moving in when we got married. Initially our relationship, particularly during the early years of our marriage, was turbulent. It was a process of getting to know each other, an adjustment.

Eleven months after we got married, our daughter Katty was born in Edenbridge, Kent, in the United Kingdom. My dad's younger brother was living there at the time and I travelled to stay with him so our child could be born in the UK as I had been. Two and a half years later, our son Mustapha was born in Ascot, also in the United Kingdom.

The tides started to turn. In a second marriage and still young, now with three children, I was weary of Byes' too much partying. He did not act like the head of the household who is supposed to take care of responsibilities for his family.

He would leave the house in the morning and return home late at night or the wee hours of the next morning, leaving me to take care of the home and our children. This was the standard routine during the first ten years of our lives together. This was not how I had envisioned our marriage or our relationship.

We spent a lot of time arguing and fighting over his irresponsible behavior. I complained to Byes and the more I complained, the later he returned home. Whenever I tried to get a friend or relative to speak with Byes, to tell him to take his responsibilities as a father and husband seriously, I was advised that I should be patient and should not expose my husband or my matrimonial problems outside of my matrimonial home. I was assured that over time, he would change. I should find a way of resolving it with him: trying to consistently please him and make him happy was one of the suggestions I often received. That is what is expected of my role as a wife.

I did find consolation from my father-in-law. He was in his early eighties, a very pious religious man and an elder in his local mosque. I used to prepare okra soup every Saturday to share with my parents and my in-laws, as well as our home. (A local traditional dish mostly prepared in The Gambia, Nigeria, Sierra Leone and Ghana, the main ingredients were shredded okra, palm oil, meat, seasoning, and assorted seafood.) I would send the traditional dish of okra soup to my parents' house during lunchtime. My father-in-law always preferred to come pick theirs up. He would arrive a couple of hours before the meal was done and would engage in keeping my company as he waited. My father-in-law became my mentor, adviser, spiritual teacher and guide. The relationship I could not build with my husband, I had with my father-in-law. He was open, non-judgmental, humble and honest. I found comfort in seeking and receiving his advice and I trusted him.

But even he could not help me in my marriage. The status quo at home in The Gambia condoned men to do as they pleased and not be challenged.

I sincerely did not want to go through another divorce and become yet another statistic at my young age. In desperation, some family and friends suggested I visit local seers, supposed spiritual and medicine men and women to use charms to get my husband to be more responsible and stay at home with the children and me. I spent a lot of money on these traditional medicine men, believing the charms and potions would work and bring my husband back to his senses.

These things just do not work.

Throughout the years, we were still married and we still lived together, but hardly saw or spent time together. When I would leave for work in the morning, he was still in bed sleeping; when I returned from work, he was gone. When he returned home I was about to get up and get ready for work and get the children ready for school. My husband was not physically abusive towards me. But at the time, even that would have been more welcomed than the emotional pain of neglect that I endured. I felt emotionally abandoned.

There was nowhere I could go to cry for help and explain what I was going through. The elders would have advised me as a woman to stay in the marriage and bear the pain for the sake of the children.

Now I had accumulated enough anger in me. I felt betrayed by my husband. I never forgave my parents for what they did to me growing up. I blamed my younger sister for telling on me and for always trying to be the "Miss Goody Two Shoes" that my parents would compare me with. I carried a heavy load of excess baggage.

To me, all the people who were supposed to love and protect me had betrayed me. I felt alone, bitter and angry.

YEARNING FOR THE UNKNOWN

In 1998, I answered the Muslim holy call to perform the Hajj pilgrimage in Mecca, the Kingdom of Saudi Arabia. The Hajj pilgrimage is one of the requirements of the five pillars of Islam. This practice is customarily done when one is a lot older and more matured. I was just thirty-one years old. Family and friends who had performed the pilgrimage were more religiously pious, had more money, came from more religious background than I did. People could not believe it when they heard that I was going to take this holy step. I don't know what happened or what got into me. I just had the urge to perform the Hajj.

I later came to realise that having a lot of money did not necessarily qualify one to "be called upon" on the Holy Pilgrimage. Neither did praying five times a day and being extremely pious and religious. It became clear to me that when it was your time, when the right time came along, re-gardless of age, gender, status, or wealth, the call will come upon you. It is believed that only when that time comes you will receive a knowing from God, a feeling that it is time to go on the pilgrimage and perform the Hajj. That is what happened to me.

At the time, my sister-in-law Katty and her husband were residing in Riyadh, in Saudi Arabia where my brother-in-law was the Military Attache for the government of Senegal. It was therefore not difficult to meet the administrative and visa requirements, thus making the process easy and convenient, travelling with them to Mecca and Medina.

In my culture, most people would pay for their parents to go to Mecca first but my dad had already performed the Hajj in Mecca. My mum accompanied him as far as Jeddah, but no farther. Non-Muslims are not allowed to enter the Holy City of Mecca. It is forbidden.

I paid for myself to perform this spiritual journey, and had enough funds to cover the cost for my husband to join me in the pilgrimage as well. At the time, he was not spiritually motivated and was not keen to travel. Religion was just not his thing. But he agreed to the invitation and accompanied me. The pilgrimage stirred different things within each of us. For me, my spiritual journey had just begun.

Thereafter, my ambition grew. The words from my mum that I heard while growing up haunted me, but they also inspired me to aspire to do great things. I was adamant and determined that I was not going to turn out as she had said.

I changed jobs to work in the development sector, strived in my work there for a couple of years, and then decided to take a leave of absence to pursue my Masters degree in the UK. I believe the motivation behind many of the actions I took— the pilgrimage to Mecca, the decision to do my Masters and taking on my Doctoral studies and much more—was to prove my parents wrong. Secondly, I felt the only way I could earn respect from my husband and my parents was to do something for myself without financial help and support from them.

Byes and I both agreed that it was not practically feasible for him to take care of our three children during my absence. They would stay with my mum and dad in The Gambia (even though he was also there) where they could have the added care of the home help. I would not be able to visit since I was taking a full time course and I had to work. This was a difficult decision, for me having to stay away from my children for a year, but it was a necessary step for me to take.

Because I had been born in the UK my tuition fees were home status, which helped financially. At the same time I had taken on leave of absence without salary to pursue my studies, thus, I needed money to survive as a student in the UK. I took on three menial jobs to cover my tuition, my accommodations, and my stipend. I worked at a chicken factory from 10pm to 6am, then returned to my dorm and slept for three to four hours, attended lectures until 3pm, studied in the library until 6pm and then went to work at the nearby hospital from 6pm to 9pm where I served the patients food and cleaned hospital floors. On the weekends, I worked in a care home taking care of elderly patients with dementia. This was my daily and weekly routine for nearly six months.

My husband visited twice and stayed on campus with me. When I went for lectures and work, he would cook. He also came around when I was working on my Masters thesis and helped with reviewing my drafts.

One month prior to my final exams, I began feeling intense pain and had to undergo tests at the hospital. The tests revealed a cyst growing inside one of my ovaries. I was hospitalized and underwent surgery to have it removed. A week later, I started having a fever. My temperature was high and I kept throwing up and bleeding heavily. My friends on campus were not aware of the seriousness of my situation. I went to the hospital emergency room and they told me it was normal for me to bleed sometimes after surgery. They gave me some painkillers and iron tablets and I returned to campus.

On the second week following surgery, I could not get out of bed. My colleague Leah Shibu from Tanzania, who stayed in the same dorm floor on campus as I did, came to my room to check on me. I was so scared at how I was feeling that I didn't lock my door so she was able to walk right in.

Not realizing how ill I was, as Leah entered my room she called out cheerfully, "Hey woman, where have you been? I haven't seen you around campus."

All I could do was moan, "Call 999. I am dying."

I had thrown up and messed my bed, my feet were turning grey. She grabbed my cell phone and called the emergency room. They told her I had been there a couple of days prior and that they had given me some medications; I should be okay in a day or two. Panicked, Leah hung up and called the university medical centre. The doctor on call came to my room and saw my condition.

By this time I could not speak. Leah later described how my eyes had gone all funny and that she could not see my pupils. The doctor quickly examined me and dialed 999 again to request an ambulance. She received the same message Leah had received when she gave them my details. According to Leah, they finally listened when the doctor said, "This woman is dying and if anything goes wrong I will make sure her family holds the hospital responsible. She is here alone with no family and is a student at the university."

Within minutes an ambulance arrived and I was rushed to the hospital. I had lost so much blood, I was only half conscious. Upon arrival at the hospital they rushed me to a room. I could barely hear two people saying, "Oh my God. Oh my God! Rush her to theatre!" Still half conscious, I recall being put on a stretcher and being wheeled by a bald white man.

I murmured to him that I did not want to die here. "My children," I mumbled. Mustapha was the youngest at the time. He was three years old.

I kept saying, "My children. I don't want to die."

He said to me, "Let us pray. Let us pray. Keep praying." As I entered into theatre, he handed me over at the theatre door entrance and I could faintly hear him say, "Pray, pray, pray." And that was all I could remember.

I woke up eight days after my second surgery, completely unaware I had been unconscious for that long. When I opened my eyes, I saw a nurse sitting by my bedside. I tried to speak but there were tubes in my mouth and down my throat. I was not allowed to eat for five days. There was a sign on my hospital room door that read "Nil by mouth." I was weak, going in and out of sleep, and only surrounded by colleagues, lecturers, and the Dean of my university. They would visit me every day. Somehow they were able to get in touch with my aunty Olive and uncle Mo, who had moved to live in Sandhurst, in southwest England. I was in Norwich on the northeast side of England. They also notified my husband and my parents.

Apparently, what happened was that after my first operation to remove the cyst, there was something accidentally left inside. I was told it was a piece of gauze or something. I got an infection, which sometimes happens after surgery, but mine was most certainly complicated with the mistake made in surgery. As a result of the infection, I lost one of my ovaries, one of my fallopian tubes, and my appendix. Part of my liver was also infected.

This was a terrible process for me. None of my family members were around and I relied on the love and care of colleagues, friends, and my university lecturers' support whilst in the hospital. My colleagues would take notes from lectures for me. Some would record lectures for me and bring the recordings to the hospital for me to listen to with headphones. It was time to prepare for my final exams but I was still in the hospital. The university advised that I could defer my exams and take them later in the summer.

I would hear nothing of it.

I came to the UK to do my Masters and I was bent on having that degree, come rain, come shine. I worked too hard to get to this point and was not willing to postpone my exams. If I had to be wheeled from my hospital bed to the examination hall, so be it, but this exam, I will take. And, I did. I was literally wheeled from the hospital to the university examination hall. Some colleagues cried when they saw me struggling into the examination hall. The Dean of my university offered that given the unique circumstances of my case, if for any reason I did not pass the written examination, I could retake the exams again that summer.

After the exams, and when the hospital agreed that it was now safe for me to convalesce at home, my aunt and uncle drove up to Norwich to pick me up. I stayed with them convalescing. I was still very weak, could not walk properly, could not take a bath on my own, and could not feed myself. I couldn't do anything for myself but just lie down in one place. Weeks went by and months went by. And finally the exam results were out.

I had passed. I now hold my Masters of Arts Degree in Gender Analysis in Development.

Then came the next hurdle. Given that I was out of work for a few months as a result of being hospitalized and practically incapacitated, I obviously could not work to pay my tuition and accommodation bills that I had accrued during the second and final semester. The university understandably was lenient with me and agreed on a payment plan. I would, however, not receive my Masters certificate until I paid my outstanding fees.

Fortunately there were a couple of care homes close to my aunt and uncle's house. Although the wounds from my surgery were not fully healed, I had recovered enough to take on twelve to eighteen hour shifts, shuttling from one care home to the other. I worked night shifts until I was able to pay my tuition and bills, with enough extra to buy new furnishings, household appliances, gifts and clothes for my three children who were waiting for me in The Gambia.

I was away for a year. I returned home, back to my husband and kids, having qualified for a Master's Degree, fully empowered, more determined, and altogether enthusiastic with a whole lot of confidence in myself.

THE MORE I RECEIVED

Three months after I returned home from my Masters course, I got a new job. It will be easy to say that this job was probably meant for me. I saw the advert in the local papers, although the deadline for submission of applications had already passed. Still, something inside of me urged me to pick up the phone and ascertain whether the position was still open. I was invited for an interview and a written test the next day. Three days later I got the job. This was the day the Lord had made! I could feel in my bones that I was going places.

I became Regional Coordinator for West Africa within an international non-governmental organization called Concern Universal whose programmes were humanitarian related. The assignment meant supporting The Gambia, Senegal, Ghana, Guinea, and Nigeria, requiring me to travel the length and breadth of the West African Region and beyond. I felt relevant and important. While earning a foreign currency in my own country, I became financially independent, at least to the point of being able to meet our basic needs at home. This meant I no longer had to go through the hassle I used to in order to get money from my husband to subsidize our household expenditures. I was no longer vulnerable.

Something inside of me woke up and roared. I became eager to learn as much as I could. I learned skills on negotiation, donor coordination, how to engage with refugees who were victims of conflict in the countries we supported. My regional director gave me assignments that required skills I did not yet have; he coached me and I accepted the challenge, not realizing that the skills I was gaining were for something bigger and greater to come. I didn't complain. I worked late hours, weekends, holidays. I took everything thrown at me.

I had no idea I was being watched. I couldn't have imagined that supervisors who saw more potential in me than I saw in myself were mentoring me. It never dawned on me that my director saw how much potential I had and that every new task he was presenting me was to test my ability to manage crises, to work under pressure. I rose in the organization, moving upwards and rising to different positions. I was promoted from Regional Coordinator to different positions to eventually becoming Chair of the Board of Trustees of the same organization five years later. What happened? What had I done to deserve this, I asked myself?

It is standard practice in most African cultures to give some portion of one's monthly earnings to one's parents. I remember my mum giving allowances to her mum, her grandmother and to Aunty Mama. I also remember my dad doing the same to his mother. I believe the rationale behind this was that, in most cases, uneducated parents struggle to get their children educated. It was expected, then, that once the child completes his or her education, it was fair to give back. One would obviously not want their parents to continue to toil after they struggled to get their child in the position to earn salaries. Similarly, this practice is an acknowledgement of your older relatives who may have taken care of you. In most African cultures, families lived together—aunts, uncles, cousins, etc.—in one compound. This practice is gradually changing as the nucleus family is more often practiced now. Parents are held in high esteem in Africa, especially mothers. In the Islamic Doctrine, it has been stated in the Quran that the Prophet Mohammed said that it is better to consider and give to one's mum first, second time and the third time before considering to give to one's father on the fourth consideration. This is equally strongly believed in almost all countries that practice Islam. In some cultures, it is a taboo (curse) not to take care of one's parents. African offspring would do whatever it takes to ensure their parents are well taken care of, particularly their mothers.

In some cultures, or homes, the children would assume the responsibility of paying the rent of their parents' homes, others would take the responsibilities of the utilities bills, while others would be responsible for the career or house help. And others would be responsible for the purchase of the monthly bag of rice, the staple food. Whilst still others would give a lump sum of money to their parents. The practice varies from culture to culture and from home to home.

When the funds are received, it is equally normal practice for parents to pray for their children and send blessings to them. I gave my first paycheck to my mother to have this shared amongst my aunts, uncles, grandparents and other relatives for their prayers and blessings. Initially, when I started working, my parents were not keen to accept part of my monthly paychecks. They could afford to take care of themselves, and I figure they did not want this practice to be some form of pressure on me. At the end of the month when I would come to give my mum and dad their allowances, my dad would often say, "You have a young family and you need this money more than we do, so use it to take care of your family." I suppose my father felt that they were already comfortable and would rather give us money and help us out rather than the other way around. The money was not much in those days; it was more symbolic. My mum would take her part and would always pray for me. And this continues. Sometimes she would pray so deeply, it made me emotional and cry. After my consistent insisting, Dad finally gave in to my plea and accepted the money I gave him from my paycheck. I have a feeling Mum must have advised him to.

Over the years from the first time I shared my paycheck with my parents, each time I had a pay raise or got promoted, I increased my parents' allowances. In fact, it was always when their allowances increased that they knew I had a promotion or a pay raise. I noticed that the more my salary increased and

I increased their allowances, the more prayers and blessings I received from them, and the more successful my professional career increased. The more abundance I received, the more I flourished in my professional career and in my life.

I continued consistently the practice of giving allowances to both my mum and dad separately until my father left this earth. After his death, I doubled my mother's allowance, giving her what I used to give my father in addition to hers. My professional career and life continued to blossom. I had my work and focused all my energy on my work, which naturally impressed the different bosses I worked for.

This was all the motivation I needed considering the misery in my matrimonial home.

Many would wonder why I stayed in the marriage, having gone through the emotional trauma with my husband. He was not a violent person and was not physical. He was also not confrontational. He had a heart of gold although stubborn and just did what he wanted to do without arguing. To be honest he does not get angry. He is just playful.

My husband is a good man. He is kind and generous but was known to be irresponsible, as my family had been forewarned before our wedding. As a young man, he was a footballer and well-known athlete. He actually represented The Gambia in several sports disciplines. I did not know of him while he was doing these sports, neither had I heard about him. Yet many knew him. If not facially, they had heard his name. As a result, his fame may have gone to his head, especially being a young sports hero receiving all the attention that he had.

I stayed in the marriage because I love him and I know he loves me. He was and remains very supportive in my academic and professional life, as shown by his visits to the UK during my Masters studies when he helped review my drafts for my thesis. As my career began to develop, he encouraged me and would sometimes accompany me during my official missions. He never complained when we would have to relocate to different countries as a result of my work and helped me entertain my official guests in the house. Today, if I had to live my life again, I would still want to live my life with him and all his flaws.

During my emergency surgery during my Masters studies in the UK in 2001, the doctors had removed one of my ovaries and one of my fallopian tubes that had rotted as a result of the infection. The doctors further explained that my right ovary and right tube, although not completely damaged like the left ones, were partly infected. As such, I would no longer be able to have any more children. I explained that this was okay as I already had three children anyway.

So when eight years later, I took ill, the thought of another child was the furthest thing from my mind. In fact, I was diagnosed with malaria. The doctor prescribed the standard treatment dose for the malaria but I did not get better. My maid boiled *neem* leaves for me to drink to clear out the malaria, I had injections, I took tablets, but nothing could stop this malaria.

My husband suggested that if I did not get better, it would make sense for me to travel to the UK for a more thorough check from the doctors there. But first, he said, "Let us try one more time again with our doctor." This time my doctor recommended we test for pregnancy. I explained that I could not be pregnant because I was still on my period, I was on the pill, and the doctors in the UK had informed me after my major surgery that my right ovary and tube were no longer functioning. He decided that we tray a scan anyway.

"Well," the doctor said once he had the scan in focus over my abdomen, "Here is what the malaria has been all the time. There are the legs and fingers . . . " and so on and so forth. Given that my doctor was always joking and teasing me, I didn't believe him. I turned to look at the monitor and lo and behold, there was a baby, already about four to five months' developed.

I started to cry. I had given away my baby clothes, my pushchair, everything. Our youngest, Mustapha, was already eight years old and I had promised him he was "my chatt" (meaning he will remain the last born). I was just about to kick-start my professional career, having concluded my Masters

and starting to advance in roles at my workplace. A *baby???*
Yup, indeed. A baby.

Given that all my other children were born in the UK, we
decided I would return to the UK to have this baby as well. I
did not want him being the odd one out. And besides, "It will
be easier if we all carry British passports," I'd argued. Unfortunately, we were not sure of my expected date of delivery.
We could not tell for sure how far along I was because there
was no last menstrual date. The best we could guess was to
go with the estimated dates from the scan which showed that
we had time to attend my sister Lu's wedding in California. I
would then travel on to the UK thereafter until the baby was
ready to be born.

We arrived in the USA, early enough for me to spend time
with my friend Jarra who insisted that we stay in the USA to
have the baby. On Jarra's birthday, we all went to Red Lobster
for dinner that evening to celebrate her birthday. A few hours
after dinner my waters broke. Too early, we were not expecting
the child around this time; or at least we thought.

Strangely, my waters were greenish in color. That did not
sound right. Jarra and her husband drove Byes and me to the
hospital where my contractions started quickly. The timing
was getting closer and closer. I heard one of the doctors say,
"The baby is getting distressed; we need to do a C-section."

My fourth child, Samsudeen, was born on 30 November
2004, a very sick baby. He had swallowed meconium, causing
fluid in his lungs and an infection. The moment he was born
via C-section, Samsu was taken straight to the intensive care
unit. I was not allowed to touch or feed my baby for a whole
month. I asked Byes to go and represent us at Lu's wedding in
California. After I was discharged from the hospital, I would
go to see our infant son at the ICU every single day.

Samsu was covered in tubes all over his body. Not once did
he open his eyes or move or sigh. I would sit in the nursing
room and pump breast milk, which they would use to pass
through his tubes. There were a couple of other babies in the
ICU, one whose mother passed during childbirth and the other

whose parent did not want to breastfeed. I was like a factory supplying milk to all these babies in the ICU, including mine.

I would sit by Samsu's incubator crib and sing or talk to him, but I was not allowed to touch him. I prayed to God for Samsu. I prayed that if he was to live and suffer, that God should take him. One month of not opening his eyes, not moving, nothing. I said to one of the doctors who passed by, "I will give anything to hear my baby's voice. Anything."

She smiled and said, "You will regret you ever said that."

One day, as I sat by his crib I started to cry. A couple whose baby was in the ICU crib right next to Samsu's turned to me and asked if they could pray for him. I said yes. They started praying and went on and on and on, as tears streamed down my cheeks. The next day, I was told the baby with the praying parents was better and they had left earlier that morning. I sat in my usual chair next to Samsu's crib. All of a sudden I heard him make a little noise like "hmmm." I screamed with joy in the ICU until they had to take me out so as not to startle the other babies.

Samsu opened his eyes and refused to sleep again. One month to the day he was born, he was circumcised at the hospital and a couple of days later I was told I could take him home. Today, this miracle baby of ours has influenced change in his father's behaviour. Our miracle baby turned Byes into a dad and has become his dad's best friend.

IT WAS THE DAY

In 2006, as the political situation continued to become more and more uncertain and fragile in The Gambia, I felt the need for change. I decided that I could no longer stay in the country for economic, personal and political reasons, finding it difficult to live off of uncertainties.

My husband did not have a full time job. He had a physical security business that was not bringing in a regular income. With three children at Marina International School and Samsu, now a year and a half, in a private kindergarten, we struggled to meet school fees deadlines. We were always behind with settling our bills, utility payments, and others.

I decided I would leave with the children and find a new job with greater opportunities in the UK. My husband stated that he would not join us to live in the UK. That he thinks it best for him to stay in The Gambia and manage his security and other businesses. We agreed that he would come visit us regularly. I was fine with the agreement. The children, now 18, 11, 8 and a toddler, and I moved from The Gambia to the UK where I would become the sole breadwinner for the family.

There was now no stopping me. The Gambia was too small for my hunger and thirst to excel. I relocated to the UK with no plans and got the first, actually only, job I applied for, as if the amazing job were waiting for me. Within two months after I arrived in the UK, I was working interchangeably for a project hosted by three of the most reputable international organisations in the development sector—Oxfam, Action Aid and Save the Children—in the UK. A month later, I bought my first car for myself in the UK. Shortly thereafter, I had secured a four-bedroom *maisonette* for my children and me to live in. The children had settled in their new schools and I was clicking the air miles.

Two months after the children and I left, my husband called and said he was moving over to join us, that he could not cope being alone, and that he felt he needed to be with his family. When Byes realised that the marriage might just end, particularly when I made the decision to return to the UK with our children and without him, he finally acknowledged that he could no longer afford to allow his irresponsible behavior and his ego to ruin his marriage and lose his family. I had started to change and I was growing and maturing and he realised this. At long last he also started to change.

Soon after Byes joined us in the UK, he asked if I could let him have Samsu. It was difficult for my husband to find a job in the UK, or rather, a job that he would want, particularly at his age. At forty-eight years old, chances of finding an office job were slim. The kind of jobs that were available to him were security guard, cab driver and other menial jobs that he did not want to take on. He considered that given I had a job with a salary that could sustain us, it would be cheaper for him to be a stay-at-home dad. And besides, I travelled extensively as a project manager for the Commonwealth Education Fund (CEF). The program covered sixteen commonwealth countries in Africa and Asia. This would also save us costs of paying for childcare services.

But mostly because, he explained, the other kids didn't get to spend a lot of time with their dad; he was never home and was not around to raise them. He realised that the only way to resolve this was to share his time with the youngest, Samsu, to make up for what he lost with the older children.

"Will you let me take care of this one?" he asked.

I agreed and made a decision that if I was going to let go I could not let go half and half.

So from the age of eighteen months, Samsu was his dad's. His dad changed his diaper, bathed him, took him to play time, took him to school. I refer to Samsu and his dad as "Momo and his goat." Wherever his dad went, little Samsu was with him. As Samsu grew, his father never missed any of Samsu's classes or school events or activities. When Samsu had a school play, his dad would be there helping the class fix the lights.

I made a few attempts to try and be the disciplinarian in the house, because his dad practically lets him get away with anything. When Samsu asks for something and I say no, he will go to his dad who will obviously agree with Samsu. It is very difficult when both parents try to raise a child and one is less lenient. And then I would remind myself of my agreement to say yes and to let go when Byes asked me, "Can this one be mine?"

I pray that his dad raised him well. Samsu has a heart of gold, warm and soft. He is an extrovert, but he is spoilt and walks all over his dad. And yet . . . He helped me soften his dad, he helped me tame his dad's ego and he helped me make his dad a father. For this I am grateful and realise that, in spite of all the odds, this miracle baby came through with one nonfunctional tube and one nonfunctional ovary and he survived infected lungs for a purpose: to save my marriage.

Six months after my family and I moved to the UK, I celebrated my fortieth birthday on 24 March 2007. Forty was a milestone for me. Life was working out for me: I had a good job, one I enjoyed, four healthy children, and my relationship with my husband and my parents had improved. By this time, my mum and I had become best of friends. After my second marriage, she became my best friend and my support structure. Our relationship changed towards the extreme opposite of what it had been when I was a child and teenager still living at home. Sometimes we would be on the phone for two to three hours exchanging notes with the challenges we had with our husbands.

I was content with my life, but I was not at peace with myself.

I was very particular about what the neighbors, people or other family members perceived of us if we did not dress well, or did not behave in a ladylike or gentlemanly manner, just like mum did with us growing up. Quality was of the essence for me. Some of my friends referred to me as Mrs. Bucket (pronounced Bouquet) as Haisen of the British comedy *Keeping Up Appearances* would say.

Everything had to be in order around me; everything had to be spotless. My husband used to complain during our early years of marriage that our bedroom and bed looked so neat that he sometimes felt uncomfortable sitting on the bed. With three boys at the time, plus my husband, and a daughter whom at the time was more or less a "Tom Boy," I thought I was going crazy when I would walk into the house from work to find bits and pieces of socks and underwear scattered on the floor and staircases, the kitchen a mess, dishes not done, etc. I started to have panic attacks.

It got so bad that I had to see a psychologist in the UK when I could no longer cope with keeping my home as tidy as I would want to. The psychologist gave me an assignment. She told me to take deep breaths when I enter the house and just walk over the mess and go to my room without saying a word.

"Huhh??" I said, "I will definitely have a heart attack."

This was one experiment I was not comfortable trying. She nudged and I finally agreed to try it. When I walked into the house the next time, I felt like I was going to suffocate. I half closed my eyes and told the family that I will have my dinner upstairs, not wanting to go downstairs and be tempted to start picking things up. Strangely, I did not die; neither did the world come to an end. Eventually I was able to give them chores to do before any meal or before they could go out on Saturdays and Sundays when they had activities planned with their friends. There was also a caveat: no pocket money if the house was not tidy, the dishes not done and the house not vacuumed.

The counselor was helping me with my obsession of cleaning and working—Mum's influence had rubbed off on me—and I had proven to those who thought I couldn't or wouldn't make it, that I could, and I did. But I was still filled with pain. To make matters worse, I felt I was the only one carrying all this pain and no one else. I remained filled with bottled-up anger that was affecting my relationship with my children and my husband. My husband, now a completely changed man, had tried to make attempts for us to start a clean chapter in our lives since we had moved to a new environment. And I had refused. I wanted him to also feel the hurt I had gone through. Even though my relationship with my parents and husband had improved, I longed to let go of the pain I still held inside of me.

My husband and children bought a birthday cake with candles to celebrate my fortieth birthday. Surprisingly, the first thought that came to my mind when they asked me to make a wish before I blew the candle, was *Peace*. I had grown weary of carrying the excess baggage of hurt and anger that I'd been dragging along with me. I was tired of being tired and I knew that carrying these grudges was not helping my health. I admitted to myself I would be ungrateful with life if I continued to play the victim.

It was on this day that I prayed and gave thanks to God for all the glory and abundance in my life. It was the day I made a promise to God and to myself, the day I made the bold decision that from that day henceforth, "I choose not to carry the excess baggage of anger, hatred, bitterness or negativity." It was the day I said to myself for the first time in my life, "Oley, I forgive you for carrying all that anger with you over these years. I forgive you for making all these assumptions that you were not loved by your parents or your husband and that you needed their love to be happy." It was the day that I decided I will no longer carry the shame of my parents beating me and my father cutting off my hair and making me the public joke amongst my teenage peers. It was the day that I chose to forgive myself for carrying such anger and hatred in me because I felt I was being emotionally and psychologically abused by my husband. It was the day I told my husband and my parents that, after forgiving myself first, that I forgave them.

I made a tremendous decision on my fortieth birthday. In spite of all the pain I had suffered, I declared that from this day forth, I would be good, think good, feel good, do good and say good. If I had known that this was how light and at peace I was going to feel for just saying these things and meaning it from my heart, I would have said it a long time ago. I figure everything happens at the right time.

In early 2009, three years after my family and I relocated to the UK, my dad took ill and was diagnosed with cancer. My father was diabetic, he had high blood pressure, and seemed to have attracted every ailment that could possibly affect an aging man. Dad had been in the hospital in The Gambia for a whole month prior. When it was evident that dad's health was not improving, we arranged to have Mum and Dad come over to the UK and stay with us so Dad could get better medical attention and care. My parents stayed with us for eight months.

When they first arrived at the airport, I did not recognize my dad. He could not walk; he could not talk. He could not even recognize us. I felt pain seeing my dad like this. A man who was so proud. A man who had the energy to fight Goliath, little as he was. A man well respected and admired by his family, friends, peers and society. This man was now like a feeble little child having to have everything done for him.

I saw this opportunity to nurse and care for my dad as a blessing. I was blessed that I was able to have my parents stay with us so we could help release some of the burden of caregiving from my mum, a burden that had been so heavy on her that she aged. I was blessed to have been able to nurse and care for both my parents. I was blessed to have been born in the UK and as a British citizen send for my ill father all the way from Africa so he could receive medical care in my home and with my family in the UK to help care for him.

As I had made the decision to let go of my past, I had the opportunity to reconcile with my dad, particularly when his health was slowly improving in the UK. We had the opportunity to talk about all the anger and grudges I held inside of me. He asked for my forgiveness and expressed that at the time he was doing what he felt as a parent was the best for his child, to raise me to grow up to be a decent and fine young woman. He expressed how he also carried pain and regret whenever he saw me with my hair cut off so short, how he also carried that shame with him until now. He asked for forgiveness and I asked him for forgiveness. We forgave each other. We ironed out all that we had bottled up inside of us. He explained that perhaps if he had not been so tough on me, I probably would not have turned out so successful and happily married with a husband who was so caring and loving. He told me how blessed I was and how proud he was of me. We both cried. I was glad I had the opportunity to vent everything I held inside of me with my dad. I felt light. I felt at peace. I was proud of myself. I felt the love glow inside of me.

A special bond cemented between my father and me after that. I was favored first to have had this opportunity to exchange forgiveness with my father and ask for his forgiveness.

During that same year, Queen Elizabeth II, Queen of England, hosted a reception at Buckingham Palace in honor of the organization I worked for, to say thank you for a program well delivered. What an elevated feeling for my colleagues and me! Who would have thought, *me*, in Buckingham palace? With the Queen of England herself? In honor of our work? I requested a special invitation for Mum and Dad to attend the reception at the Palace and meet the Queen as well. The request was to grant a dying man his last wish. They did receive the invitation, but at the time Dad was too weak to even sit on a bed, let alone go to the palace. My husband and I attended, together with my colleagues and their spouses.

My dad, who had been certified to have only two to three weeks' maximum to live, started to gain weight. He went for long walks accompanied by my son Omar who was then twenty-one years old. He took himself to the hospital for his medical routine checks and put on so much weight that all his clothes were tight for him.

My father lived for five more years after he had been medically certified as a "lost cause" with only a few weeks left to live. The doctor who had told my dad he did not have long to live was amazed when Dad walked into his office six months after that dismal diagnosis.

"What happened?" the doctor asked.

Dad responded, "Good food with a lot of prayers, love, and care from family."

MY COURTSHIP WITH ABUNDANCE

The program I was working on in the UK ended in 2008. Oxfam, one of the host organizations, offered me a permanent position as a Global Program and Policy Adviser on gender equality based in Oxford, coincidentally the city where I was born. Initially, I started off filling in for a colleague on maternity leave as a Global Gender Adviser within the Humanitarian Department. This required engaging on gender issues within humanitarian settings, such as the cyclone in Myanmar Burma, which led to my visiting Myanmar to support the Oxfam program there. Similarly, we helped with aid following the flooding in Pakistan, the earthquake in Haiti, amongst others.

During that year, I decided to embark on furthering my academic career by aspiring to pursue my Doctoral studies, totally funding myself for my post-graduate study. This was one of the most challenging journeys I had yet to undertake. I was living in the United Kingdom, raising a family, married, working full time, traveling literally six months of the year, commuting 100 miles to and from work and commuting another 150 miles to and from my university. I was spending too many hours driving, I was working all night reading and writing on my research thesis and travelling around the world. It became difficult to focus. I had no life, no time for my family; and it was taking a toll on me. In truth, I almost had a nervous breakdown. The thought of it now scares me.

It was then that I decided that working and raising children

in the UK without help was not the best of ideas, especially
for one who has been used to having three to four helping
hands in The Gambia. It is normal practice in The Gambia
to have two to three house help at home, sometimes more. In
my matrimonial home, I had a babysitter who was responsible
for taking care of the children. She'd bathe them, feed them,
help them get ready for school, tidy their bedroom and keep
an eye on them whenever my husband and I had to go to work
or go out. Another house help was responsible for preparing
the meals, mostly lunch and dinner, as well as going to the
market to buy the groceries. This person was also responsible
for cleaning the house. Whilst the kids were at school, and we
at work, she would first start with the cleaning of the house
from around 9am, cleaning until noon when she would start
preparing the lunchtime meal ahead of the children returning
home from school around 2pm. Then she would begin prepa-
rations for dinner, setting the table in preparation for our 6pm
arrival. She would prepare dinner and have it all wrapped up
and set up, waiting for us on the dining table.

We also had a laundry lady who hand washed the laundry
for all of us (my husband, the kids and myself), every day.
After the washing she hung them up on the clothesline to dry.
Because of the warm weather, the clothes dried quickly and
she would iron and separate everyone's laundry, delivering
them to the different rooms. The house help responsible for
the children would sort out the kids' clothes in the drawers
and I would usually sort out my husband's and mine. We
also had a day caretaker/gardener who was responsible for
cleaning the compound every day. He'd weed the garden and
water the plants and serve as day guard of the house while the
house helps were working behind and inside the house doing
the chores. We had a driver who was responsible to take the
kids to school in the morning and pick them up after school
and drop them off after school and take them back to school
if they had any after school activities. He was also responsible
for running errands. I would generally drive myself to work
and my husband would also drive himself to work.

Having been used to this lifestyle of having local house help made it more difficult for my husband and me in the UK. The United Kingdom adheres to the International Labour Organisation (ILO) regulation against importation of maids into the UK. There were cleaning and babysitting services available in the UK, but these were officially registered babysitters. One also would have to contract a registered cleaning company that offered services to clean houses. These were very expensive. For laundry, one would either have a washing machine in their home or go outside to the launderette services.

Help services in most African countries is very cheap. Most of my house helps lived in our home with us during the week and would go home for the weekends on Saturdays. Some would even tell us they do not wish to go home. Living with us meant we were responsible for feeding them, we provided accommodation for them, and they saved on daily transportation costs. I had a couple of house helps who would request I keep their salaries for six months until they would have a sizeable amount, enough to go to their homes in the countryside or to the neighbouring Cassamance region in Senegal. Once they had accumulated enough pay, they would then take two to three weeks off to go visit their parents and would buy oils, rice and other food to take to their family.

Because my husband had a physical security company, we had a security guard who was responsible for the security of the compound at night. It was not expensive to have these services. Now, I am made to understand that this practice is changing and the services of house helps in The Gambia is becoming very expensive, but at the time this type of home help was affordable and common. I grew up familiar with these services in my parent's home, and I missed them terribly in the UK.

It was time to find another job outside of the UK where I could easily get some help at home with the children, and where the weather was more favorable. I was tired of running around, working, picking up the kids and dropping them off, doing grocery shopping in the rain. For me, living in a country in which the weather was always rainy was an inconvenience.

It was also more difficult for the kids to go out and play in the park and playgrounds without an adult needing to be around to keep an eye on them. This was not the case back home in The Gambia. Kids could be out visiting their friends as young as eight years old. They could be in the streets or park playing football without the need for adult supervision. Security for children in our African community was less of an issue than in the UK. Yes, it was time to look for a job in Africa. I could finish my Doctoral studies remotely.

In 2010, I applied for a job in Kenya as Deputy Executive Director for a Pan African Organisation called the Forum for African Women Educationalists (FAWE). I was invited for an interview for the position of Deputy Executive Director. When I arrived for an interview for that position, I was instead offered the position of Executive Director. I had not applied for the Executive Director position, nor had I even seen the terms of references. Along with a generous salary came perks, like living facilities for the Executive Director, education grants for my children, medical insurance coverage, amongst others. I had found my dream job in a dream country with a lucrative package, just waiting for me to own. I accepted the offer and moved to Kenya.

My family joined me six months later and we settled well in Nairobi. My husband did not work in Kenya either, but continued his role as stay-at-home dad while I worked. He voluntarily opted to coach a local football club, and other times he was engaged in Samsu's school and social activities. My husband loves sports, any kind of sports. Actually, he is ad-dicted to sports and I would usually refer to myself as a "sports widow." Thus he would spend most of his time watching soccer when it was the season, or cricket when it was the season, or tennis when it was the season, or the grand prix, or American football or baseball or basketball. As a result, this kept him up most nights glued to the TV. He had to have his own TV with super sports channels so he could watch TV almost 24/7 and I mean literally. He could be lying on his special lounger watching sports on TV without moving or wanting to eat.

I got my inspiration from traveling and meeting young girls through my job. Just a few months into my new role as FAWE Executive Director, I made a visit with our team to Kadiajo in the Masai area. Some friends of FAWE were visiting us from the USA, and we wanted to show them one of our FAWE Centres of Excellence. On the long drive from Nairobi to Kadiajo, we passed some Masai women and young girls walking, accompanied by a man. They seemed to have recently left the school that we were just about to visit. When we arrived at the school, I casually enquired whether they had held a parent-teacher meeting that morning as we had seen what looked like some parents and children just coming from the school.

The head teacher casually explained that these mothers had brought their daughters to the school to keep them away from their fathers who had already accepted their bride prices to marry them off. The mothers wanted the school to keep the girls since it was a boarding school and a "safe house."

"So what happened?" I enquired.

"Well," she replied, "We cannot take them because they do not have money to cover the cost of the tuition, uniform, and sanitary facilities. Unfortunately, we had to send them back home."

The first thought that came to my mind was: *Send them back to their fathers so they could be married off?* I asked the head teacher how much it would cost to keep these girls in school for a year. I don't quite remember what she said but it was something around $35-$40USD for everything they needed.

I opened my purse and emptied some Kenyan shillings and a few US dollars on the head teacher's desk. Our visitors also opened their wallets, but because they carried credit cards, they didn't have much US cash on them. We put all of our money together, including the coins and every currency we had, and asked the head teacher if it would be enough to hold onto until we returned to Nairobi and could send the rest of the money.

"Actually," she answered, "what you have here should cover the cost of all three of them for a year."

I yelled, "Quick! Go call them back."

Someone ran after the girls and their mothers and told them to come back to the school. (I just got goose pimples all over. I always do when I explain this story). They had walked all the way to Kadiajo from the Tanzania border and were headed back home. As soon as the group of travelers returned, I looked into these girls' eyes and started to cry. I was the Executive Director of the organization that supports this Centre of Excellence and Safe House for girls in the African continent, thirty-four countries, and we had just saved the lives of these three girls.

The principal handed the money to the mums to go to the nearest town with the girls and buy the required necessities. I decided we would wait until they returned. About three hours later the girls showed up in uniforms, carrying their tiny suitcases filled with the necessary toiletries and requirements to stay in school. I could not fully imagine how our arrival at that perfect time transformed the lives of these girls forever. The mums were crying, I was crying, and the young girls, I believe twelve, thirteen and fourteen years old, just stood there staring at us.

Although I had studied gender equality and women's rights, and also worked in these areas, this experience was the first wake up call for me and I shall forever remember it. It was then that it dawned on me that not enough was being done to address the issues of girls' education in Africa. That was the day my mission for girls' education started. As I travelled around and across the continent, I encountered too much rhetoric on the issues of girls' education. It became clear to me that we needed to educate everyone—from the political leaders to the farmers—about the importance of girls' education. One only needs to travel the length and breadth of the African continent to see what is happening to girls and how their lives are being used for the survival of their families.

As we visited schools around the continent, advocating for girls' education and women and girls' rights in Africa, I enjoyed seeing the excitement and hope in the faces of the young girls.

I had found my passion. Working to support young women inspired and motivated me to grow even more. I was so passionate about my work, it no longer felt like a job. I listened to success stories of women and girls who had previous challenging experiences being in education and to young adolescent girls struggling in their communities who had overcome these challenges. I watched young girls who when I first met them were shy and had low self-esteem, later stand up and speak with confidence, expressing what they wanted for themselves. I'd listen to women talk about their coping strategies, how they come together and lift each other up. These stories motivated and inspired me. They still do.

I long to see the day when no individual is allowed to have her life dictated by her community. I yearn to see young women and girls rise to become leaders in their own rights, to become who they want and aspire to be. I long for the ability for us as women to be able to express our feelings in our matrimonial homes, the boardroom, in the political arena without being judged. I long to see more and more glass ceilings being broken for women and girls having their own identities rather than being associated as the "wife of". . . , the "daughter of" . . . and so on.

On one of my trips to the USA, I made a presentation as a keynote speaker at the Center for Universal Education at the Brookings Institute in Washington, DC. At the end of my presentation, I was invited for an interview about my perspective on girls' education in Africa. Someone there offered to write about me—my background and how I got to where I was. I always love to tell personal stories during my speeches and presentations especially when it relates to work.

The gentleman began by asking me a few questions about myself.

"Who is Oley Dibba-Wadda?" he asked. I responded with the usual jargon that I was the eldest daughter of . . . sister of . . . a wife, mother to four children, etc.

He persisted. "No, seriously, who is Oley Dibba-Wadda?"

Puzzled and confused, I said, "I am not sure what you mean."

So he said, "Let's discuss further on this after you return to Nairobi."

As soon as I returned to Kenya, I called my mum and dad to tell them about this man's interest in writing a book about my story. I asked them more questions about their parents and ancestors, assuming this was the information the man wanted to know about me. My parents shared as much as they could remember and I took a large number of notes, preparing to share with this man during our next follow-up call. But apparently this was not what he wanted.

He asked me again. "Who is Oley Dibba-Wadda?" I started getting irritated, not with the interviewer as much as with myself because I couldn't answer his question. Since my job was my passion I poured myself into it, with the nagging question in the back of my mind. *Who is Oley Dibba-Wadda?*

What I didn't realise was that with all the excitement and demand of my job, I did not notice the wear and tear it was causing to my body. I worked nonstop. Sometimes in the middle of the night my husband would be lying next to me sleeping, and there I'd sit in my nightdress or pajamas on a video having a virtual meeting with someone in the USA. I just went on like a machine. On and on I went.

Soon the demands started to wear me down. I was getting tired—too tired to eat, too tired to climb the stairs, too tired to even talk. Then to crown it all, insomnia kicked in. My uncle and his family were living in Kenya at the time and he scheduled an appointment for me to meet with a cardiologist. Off I went for my appointment. They did many different tests on me, from MRI to ECG to ultrasound to nutrition, the whole works. Ultimately, the warning came that if I do not slow down, the next time I will not be walking into the hospital, but that it will be my corpse being transported.

Another test also revealed I had multiple fibroids as well that were equally contributing to my fatigue. I underwent surgery and was referred to a nutritionist for advice on changing my diet. Unlike some, surgery was not a problem for me. But the advice to eat healthy? That was not likely. My motto was: "I am a West African. We are carnivorous. I live off rice and meat and will only do chicken as a last resort." Greens and beans were not my idea of food.

Three days following my surgery, I was discharged from the hospital and confined to bed at home for three weeks. *Three weeks? For me?? A self-confessed workaholic?* That was the worst punishment I could receive. The doctor instructed my colleagues at the office not to allow me into the office, not to respond to my emails, and not to copy me on any email communication thread. My once always-buzzing mobile phone turned dormant. My husband had wanted to keep it so I could rest. The look I shot him was enough to demonstrate the damage already caused by the doctor, so he reluctantly let me keep it. Every so often, I would sneak my phone out from under my pillow, where I kept it for safekeeping in case my husband and or children ganged up on me to take it away from me with the assumption that they were doing this in my best interest, and take a peek but mostly it remained silent due to the doctor's orders. Out of boredom, and with nothing to do, not even allowed to go downstairs, I pulled open my bedside drawer and found a book I had shoved in there a month earlier.

The book had been given to me in a cosmetics store in Westlands in Nairobi. The lady at the checkout told me that I spent enough money to qualify for their special promotion, and as such, they have a book as a gift for me. I took the book and thought nothing of it. I threw the book in the carrier bag along with the rest of the cosmetics I bought. When I emptied the bag upon arrival at home, I tossed the book in my bedside drawer and forgot about it. Until I was put on solitary confinement.

I am not a TV person. I would much rather read a book or read from the collection of Good Reads on my Kindle. Or listen to music. Because I was confined to bed with nothing else to do, given that my options were limited, I decided to read the book I had tossed in my drawer a month earlier. The book was titled *Inspiration, Your Ultimate Calling* by Dr. Wayne Dyer. I started reading the book around 10am one morning.

I did not stop; actually, I could not put the book down, until I finally finished the book at 3am. I got out my Kindle and bought every single book by Wayne Dyer available on Amazon the next day.

That was a turning point for me.

The book brought up so many "aha" moments for me. That everything I saw, thought and felt were mostly based on what I encouraged in my mind. That to entertain peace felt like being a bird freed from a cage, that expressing love without fear was the most awesome feeling and that gratitude and forgiveness were the key to living in heaven here on earth. I think I may have read that book at least five times during my convalescent period. The second time round, I read chapters and paragraphs to my husband. I offered the book to my two eldest children to read, but they were not interested. I tried to explain the background of the book but by this time they thought I was going *kou kou* in the head with all this talk about spirituality and what not. I read a couple more of Wayne Dyer's books, *The Power of Intention* amongst others, and the universe opened up for me.

Thereafter, I started seeing everything through different eyes, through a different set of lenses. My soul had opened up with no intention of becoming dormant again. Ever.

QUEST FOR LIFE'S PURPOSE

I returned to work after my three weeks of strict bed rest. With my new knowledge of myself and my physical limitations, I would leave the office at 6pm and head home. I began to read more and more books by Wayne Dyer and when I exhausted those, I read Neal Walsch's books on *Conversations with God, Books 1, 2 and 3.* Not long after, Iyanla Vanzant's name popped up. I read all her books, then started going online to watch her programmes on the Oprah Winfrey Network. Before I knew it, I had read Iyanla's books twice—every single one of them until her most recent release in 2016. *Trust.* I moved on to Eckhart Tolie and all his books. On a mission to Canada a colleague was listening to an audio book. I asked her what the title of the audio book was and she said it was titled *Re-inventing the body, Resurrecting the Soul* by Deepak Chopra. So I once again picked up my Kindle and ordered all of Deepak Choprah's books at the time. Soon someone else mentioned Robin Sharma's book *The Monk Who Sold His Ferari.* I searched online for the book through Amazon but found nothing. The yearning for a copy of this book became a mission for me. I decided to look for a copy of the hard cover of the book in every airport I transited through. Finally, I found just one copy at Schipol Airport in Amsterdam. Throughout the flight back to Nairobi, I continued reading.

Reading inspirational and motivational personal development books became my sole favourite past time. Before I knew

"

it, I had bought over thousands of books on Amazon. Each time I ordered something for my Kindle, a notice came up from Amazon that reads "people who bought this book, also bought this." I would buy the recommended book as well. Someone also suggested Rhonda Byron's *Magic, Secret and the Power* and I bought them all too. I reached about 2,000 books and had now started spreading the word about the positive impact these books were having on my life. I started recommending the books to my mother, friends, and anyone who dared to listen. I ended up buying a Kindle for everyone in my entire household, including my mum, and set up a shared account in which all the books I had on my Kindle could be read by any of my family members, irrespective of what part of the globe they were in. Even my eight-year-old son at the time had a Kindle. What I was learning had to go viral and it must start with my family first.

Life was teaching me so many lessons and I was eager and open to these lessons. As the saying goes: "when the student is ready, the teacher arrives." This is precisely what was happening to me. We actually have this in my local language, in *Wolof: Aduna, hel, bott, jamano.* Meaning, in life one needs to be conscious, needs to be observant and needs to appreciate that everything in life is just moments and this is so true. I would spend my entire weekends on You Tube listening to these inspirational speakers. The more I read, watched and listened, the more my life was changing. What I had not understood was that the day I made the declaration on my fortieth birthday to be good, think good, feel good, do good and say good, I had opened myself up to the universe to bring more and more inspirational teachers, books and individuals into my life.

I started coming across like-minded people who read similar books and we shared stories about the abundance we were receiving. As my life changed, I was attracting the right people in my life. My relationship with my husband and children blossomed, my relationship with my parents blossomed, my career blossomed, my finances blossomed and my confidence grew more and more. My concerns about what people thought of me grew less and less.

One evening as I was reading one of my usual inspirational books, I had a personal revelation. I found myself pondering: Who am I? What is my purpose in life? What am I here to do in this life? What was reflected in the book I started off reading in the first place? The book by Wayne Dyer, *Inspiration, Your Ultimate Calling*. And where do I fit into the message of the book Wayne Dyer wrote? That evening, something strange began to happen to me. I took a piece of paper and started to write down what was coming through my head. I had no idea what I was writing or why I was writing; but I was writing. It was not planned, it was not rehearsed, I did not read it from anywhere. I just blurted out on my paper as follows:

"My Life is to give and share all that I AM and all that I have to humankind. I get my Inspiration from the longing for love, the search for knowledge, gratitude for all that I AM and compassion for the living. This is my Life."

Bham!! I finally figured it out. This is who I am! At last I understood what the question was about: "Who is Oley Dibba–Wadda?"

All this time I had no clue that the many books I had been reading were signs and messages to help me discover myself. I wrote the phrase down and shared it with my husband and kids and they all separately acknowledged that this is actually who I am. This is what I lived for and this is what I did every day—at work, at home within my communities and extended families.

I called my mum and dad from Nairobi to share with them this new revelation I had just received. They both confirmed that, indeed, that is who I am. Mum reminded me of how I would steal food from her kitchen and give to our less fortunate neighbors. She reminded me about so many things I did growing up—giving away my clothes, jewelry, shoes, bags; stealing money from her purse for the poor and then saying to them, "My mum says I should give this to you." Without my truly comprehending, I had consistently wanted to be closer to those less fortunate than me. Just like Aunty Mama I would find myself showing empathy, wanting to live the same way as those who had less than our family, even with all the privileged opportunities and possibilities I had. Bringing underprivileged strangers home and claiming they were distant relatives. It also became evident to Mum and Dad that in spite of the merciless beatings I received, all the punishments, I always went back and did it again and again even though I knew what the consequences were. There had to be something.

After I put the phone down, after I finished talking to Mum and Dad, my husband and kids, I knew I had deciphered the secret code to my purpose in Life. Later, I had it written on my email signature, on my Facebook and Twitter profiles, and anything that represented me. I tried to call the guy who wanted to write my biography but could not get ahold of him. I sent him emails and excitedly wanted to share "who I was" and what I just found out, but did not receive any response from him. I was later told that he passed on. Perhaps he was not meant to write a book about me; perhaps he just briefly crossed my path for "a reason," to push me on a quest in search of my Life's purpose. Perhaps I will never know why.

But what I do know now is that I found my purpose. All along, it was my way of life. It was what I did every day of my life without realizing it.

In the meantime, Dad's health was slowly deteriorating. When I went home to The Gambia with my husband and kids in December 2012 to spend Christmas with my parents, I saw how aged my parents were becoming. It affected me deeply. I felt guilty as I admitted to myself it did not matter how much money I spent on them or what I bought for them, it could not compensate for the fact that Dad was heading downhill. Mum, as the main caregiver once again, had lost all her beauty. She had lost a lot of weight, had bags under her eyes, and even when she smiled you could tell it was too much for her.

My two younger sisters were living in Gambia at the time and they did what they could. Our parents were equally stubborn and strong headed. Mum felt it was her "cross to care for

Dad on her own" 'till the end. It was not easy for my siblings to break through. One of my sisters offered for Mum and Dad to move in with her and her family. Mum would hear nothing of it. Dad's health got better and then worse again. It went on and off. Dad was going in and out of the hospital like he was checking into a hotel. I cried. I begged Dad to slow down so we could give him the love and care both he and Mum deserved.

After the Christmas holiday our family returned to Nairobi and I decided to quit my job in Nairobi. Yes, my dream job. As the eldest child, I had a responsibility to my parents. It was not about sending them money every month or paying the medical bills. My presence was equally as important. I was quitting to go home and be near my parents in their time of need, to help my siblings sort through all of this with Mum and Dad.

I resigned after just concluding a US $17 million funding grant for FAWE. It took eighteen months to cultivate and nurture the partnership for this grant to go through and now I was not going to see the program implemented. When I handed in my resignation letter, the Executive Committee declined my resignation. They empathized and naturally, all of them being African women (who were former African ministers and academics), appreciated where I was coming from. They suggested that instead of resigning, I take a six-month sabbatical to go take care of my dad and help relieve the pressure from my mum. But I felt it would be unfair for me to lead a Pan African Organisation of that nature remotely, and besides I had no guarantee what I was going to find when I returned home. I did not know how long it would take for my dad to either get better or pass on. They understood and reluctantly agreed on a mechanism for transitioning support to my successor remotely.

By this time, news had started going round like wildfire that I was leaving FAWE. There was uncertainty about the leadership from some donors and I had to explain that a transition plan would be put in place and they can be assured that their funds will be well managed. During my notice and transition period at FAWE, I was approached by the Chair of another Pan African Organisation. Their organisation focuses on women, peace and security in Africa and she was asking me to consider taking on the role as Executive Director. She was managing the organization while at the same time serving as the Chair. In addition, she had received another assignment as a Special Envoy with the African Union Commission and was hesitant to take on the added responsibility coupled with leading the Pan African Organisation. She did not want to advertise for the Executive Director position, so naturally, I was headhunted.

I explained that my mission was not to work again, but to return home and help my mum take care of my dad. She suggested that since her organization was in Senegal, which was next to The Gambia, I could still work closer to home and spend time with my father who would be a mere 25-minute flight away. It made sense. I could still work and earn a living for my family and at the same time be able to spend quality time with my parents. I accepted the offer and moved with my husband and son, who was eight years old at the time, the only one still in the nest. We moved closer to home.

I started looking for accommodations to rent in Dakar not realizing that God's plan was not for me to rent a house to stay in, but to buy a property of my own close to the airport. I discovered a brand new settlement with an as-yet vacant complex. We were the first family to move in. Within months and after several bureaucratic processes, I had the property bought and in my name. I remained working and was able to frequently visit home and spend time with my parents. As well, I was able to arrange for my mum and dad to come over and take a break when needed because we were now just next-door by plane.

We all agreed to celebrate our first New Year's in Dakar in our new property with the entire family—my parents, my sister and her husband and children, my youngest sister, some friends. We had all been together at my parents' house for Christmas and were all packed and ready to drive to our new home in Dakar. Dad was not allowing us to go without him. He did not want to miss out on the fun. We were concerned because he was too weak and we were traveling a six- to eight-hour turbulent drive from Banjul back to Dakar by road. We weren't sure his health would be able to accommodate the rough drive over and back. We suggested he travel by air with mum and join us. He would hear nothing of it. If we were all traveling by road, he wanted to be part of the fun, music and ambiance during the drive to Dakar. So we padded him well with pillows to protect him from the bumpy roads. Dad was even more excited than we were.

New Year's 2014 was the best New Year's for me. Although we had a few panic attacks with Dad wanting to eat anything and everything we prepared, we ended the year with him even getting out of bed to dance into the New Year with us. It was something magical watching Dad dance with Mum and with his grandchildren. After the New Year celebration he insisted again that he was returning back to The Gambia by road instead of by air.

I was blessed with the opportunity to have my dad see my new property in Dakar and pray for me there and give his blessings. I also had the opportunity of visiting him often and spending meaningful time with him, listening to the assignments and tasks he wanted me to take on as the eldest if he passed on.

Two weeks before he passed, I was on a mission in the Cassamance Region of Senegal. During my routine call to check in on him and Mum, he requested I come over to The Gambia as he had some important things he wanted to discuss with me. I was due to travel to the United States for another mission so I suggested I cancel the US mission so I could come over and answer whatever it was he wanted to discuss.

He said to me on the phone, "Don't worry. Go on your mission to Washington and when you return, then come home. I need to discuss some things with you." He added, "I am not going anywhere yet. I will wait for you."

After my Washington mission, I took time off work and went back to The Gambia. Dad's condition had changed; he could no longer walk and had to be fed. It was a painful sight for me. I saw the pain in my mother's eyes as well. She was tired but insisted she would not allow anyone but herself to take care of Dad. Most nights she would not sleep. Dad was diabetic and because of the medications he was taking for the cancer, his blood sugar became low to the point where he was delirious and hallucinating. One night I suggested to Mum that we try to get a cube of sugar down him. It worked miracles. We managed to stabilize him that night. These incidences usually happened in the middle of the night for some strange reason. Some nights Dad accepted the sugar, other times he'd pinch his lips together and refuse.

During those final days, I spent quality time with my dad and knew I was blessed. He told me to take care of my siblings and bring them together. He made me promise to take care of Mum when he was gone, which I did. He could not speak well, but mustered the courage to pray for me and praise me and thank me. He told me to thank Mum for him on his behalf and that I should tell Mum she was a good wife. We once again went through the forgiveness phase. I asked for his forgiveness and told him that I forgave him for all the anger I had as a teenager.

He told me he was proud of me, of my husband and me, and that he wanted me to go follow my dreams and go back to the job I enjoyed. I told him about two prospective jobs in the pipeline that I was considering. He had suggested I take the one within the UN because he had once worked for that organization, but he listened intently as I shared with him I was not vying for that job. I admitted to him that I wanted to return back to education because that was where my passion was—working on education in Africa.

My dad, the strict father who had deprived me of teenage social outings and had forced me to study culinary arts, said something to me at that point that I had never expected. He told me he recognized that I had taken this job to be closer to home, but if I was not enjoying my job I should go back to working in the education sector where my passion was. He told me he had done what he had to do to make sure his children had the best in life and that he wanted me to do the same for my children. And then he said to me that working somewhere where my heart wasn't, just so I would be close to home, was unfair.

I returned back to Dakar having kissed Dad on the forehead and giving him a big hug and squeeze. I tried to say goodbye, but Dad refused to turn and look at me. He knew that was the last time we would see and talk to each other. I had not realised this. I promised him I would be back in another week. He squeezed my hand and I left for the airport and returned to Dakar.

A week after I left, Dad passed away on 14 April 2014. I woke up on the morning of his passing feeling chills in my body. Immediately, my sister called me that morning to say Dad had been taken to the hospital the evening before. I called my husband from the office to start packing. I was on my way home to pick him up so we could drive as there were no flights available to Banjul that day. I got home and called my sister who was at the hospital with Mum on Dad's bedside. The moment I said, "We are leaving Dakar now on our way heading for The Gambia," I heard a heave in the background and Mum and my sister shouting, "Get the doctor!" I knew that it was over. I was on the other side of the phone when Dad was certified dead.

Since Dad was Muslim, tradition followed that he could be buried as soon as can be possible. Mum promised me that she would ensure Dad was not buried until my husband and I arrived. We were all set to travel so we set off for The Gambia, accompanied by my sister-in-law who lives in Dakar, arriving home at around 2am the next morning. Dad's corpse was wrapped and stored on ice in the bathtub in the master bathroom.

That morning, we were called upon to see Dad's face one last time after the bath rites of the corpse and before his face was covered. My brother was unfortunately in the USA and could not make it. My sisters and I were blessed with an opportunity that was not normal practice, especially for women in the Muslim religion and in our society. In the Islamic religion, the body is not usually laid for people to see. Normally, in the towns and city, the body is taken to the mortuary for the religious rights of cleaning and from there straight to the mosque where only men are allowed to participate. Because our father's body was kept overnight and washed at home, we had the opportunity to pray for him and pay our last respects.

I stood in front of the corpse and praised him for being a great father and a great husband and promised him that we will not let him down. I did not cry. I was at peace with myself and at peace with dad. I had flashbacks of my childhood, of the healing and forgiveness my dad and I were able to share, and of the ten days I had with him a week earlier and felt so lucky and so blessed.

He gave the best of what he knew and what he had for his family and had gone to rest.

WHEN THE KNOWING EMERGED

The blessings from my father started pouring after his passing. I accepted a job as Executive Secretary, a position equivalent to that of Director, with another Pan African organisation on education that was hosted by the African Development Bank (AfDB).

When I first applied for the job, I told no one about it. I actually forgot about it. I applied for the position in October of 2013 and did not hear from them until February of the following year when they invited me for an interview. I went for the interview telling no one except my mum and dad (although Dad was quite ill at the time) and my husband.

The day before the interview, I took an overnight flight from Dakar to Tunis. I arrived in Tunis the morning of the interview and went to my hotel to check in and freshen up before the interview. (I do not usually sleep on airplanes so one can imagine.) When I arrived at the hotel, the receptionist told me the room would not be ready until after 1pm. My interview was at mid-day. *This cannot be happening to me,* I thought. I took some breakfast, then headed to the hotel lobby restroom to brush my teeth, wash my face with the hotel soap, freshen up with some baby wipes I fortunately had with me, changed into my interview clothes, and put on some make-up. I asked the receptionist to keep an eye on my little overnight luggage and went to the interview.

I arrived an hour early. This gave me time to sit, relax, catch my breath, say a couple of silent prayers, repeat my mantras and affirmations (I had now become a spiritual guru, or so I thought). By the time I was called in for the interview, I knew God was saying to me, "I've got your back."

I was interviewed by a panel of all men. Two were Ministers of Education representing two different African countries, one was Vice President of the African Development Bank, one was Chief Economist of the African Development Bank and the Chair of the organization—none of whom I knew. When I walked into the room and sat down opposite the panel, I felt that something Higher than myself was with me. There was a "knowing" that I could neither explain nor understand. I was calm, relaxed, and responded to the questions asked. I demonstrated so many examples of my achievements and experiences that one of the panelists said, "We have heard enough examples."

I left the interview and returned to the hotel. Now my room was ready. I checked in, slipped out of my interview clothes, took a shower and dashed into bed for a welcome rest following my overnight flight and interview. Two hours into my sleep, my hotel room phone rang. It was one of the panelists from the interview.

"We just wanted to inform you that we finally concluded the interview and you were unanimously voted 'strongly recommended' by all the panelists," the person said. "So, the good news is that you got the job and the bad news is that you are required to start yesterday."

I explained that I could not start immediately because I still work for my organization in Dakar and will be required to give at least a month's notice. I further explained on the phone that I would not be able to hand in my resignation to my current employer until I receive an official offer letter from them. Anyway, I thanked the panelist for the information and called my husband to share with him what had transpired. I tried to go back to sleep but it was impossible. *How could things just turn out like this for me?* I prayed and thanked God so many times in the hotel room that I burst out crying. A grown up professional sitting on the floor in a hotel in Tunis weeping because I was grateful to God for His favour. That evening, I took my flight back to Dakar and returned to work as if nothing happened. I had requested for two days off, so that was that.

By this time, I had no idea there was chaos at the new organization I had just concluded my interview with. I was waiting for my letter offering me a position but nothing came. Two months went by, then three, still nothing. By this time, news had started going round that I had been offered this position, it even reached my current employer at the time. But I still had not received any letter. I wondered, *How could they be talking about something like this when they have not contacted me, the candidate, to tell me officially if I was successful or not?*

News finally got to me through other friends working in the AfDB that they heard I came for an interview and was successful, but that there was a protest by one of the applicants who was at the time acting as the Officer in Charge (OiC) in the absence of an Executive Secretary. He questioned the authenticity of the recruitment process, resulting in the bank requesting an evaluation and investigation of the interview and recruitment process. An evaluation and investigation exercise was conducted twice by different ethics investigators to ascertain the authenticity of the recruitment process and both groups came up with the same findings. The interview process was transparent and I was indeed the successful candidate. Unaware that any of this was going on, I had actually started getting on with my life and putting this potential position at the back of my mind.

In June 2014, four months after the interview and a week before they wanted me to start work, I received an offer letter and a contract for my signature. I was expected to assume office on 1 July 2014. How could I? I had to hand in my notice to my current employer, which I had not done in the absence of an official offer. I ended up having to pay one month in lieu, leave within the week and assume my new duties in Tunis. I learned that when your stars are aligned, it doesn't matter what anyone does; it may stall or delay things, but if it is yours, it will come to you.

I was the first woman to occupy the position in the twenty-eight years of the organisation's existence. The package also included education grants for my children, medical insurance, diplomatic status and everything I had in my package in Kenya but at a larger scale and more. I moved to Tunis to take on my new assignment.

Sadly, in the process I had to separate temporarily from my family for a year. A large part of my responsibility was a matter of getting my team in Tunis organised and relocated to Abidjan, Ivory Coast. The African Development Bank was relocating back to Abidjan after eleven years of temporarily staying in Tunis during the conflict that had erupted in Ivory Coast at the time. My joining ADEA coincided with the bank returning. Because Samsu was already settled in school in Dakar, it did not make sense for my husband and son to join me for a year in Tunis only to have to move and find another school again in Abidjan a few months later.

It was in Tunis, whilst living alone without my family that my spiritual journey and awakening became more immersed. I had time to myself. I had time to quiet my mind, to read more, to listen to inspirational stories and speakers. I have taken a deliberate stance not to watch TV, particularly the news. The news is too negative and was sucking up my positive energy. My husband insists that it is important to listen to the news and be familiar with what is going on in the world, especially with my job, but I refuse to.

I embarked on and signed up to one of Iyanla Vanzant's 90-day "Pump up the Power" online workshops with personal tutorials from Iyanla herself. I embarked on the 7-day mental diet. I took on assignments and projects, developed affirmations. I learnt so many spiritual processes.

I also engaged a Muslim cleric to teach me the teachings of the Quran during my one-year stay in Tunis. Interestingly, he requested I read three books two months before we were to start the classes. He gave me the books in English—transliteration of the Torah, the Bible, and the Quran. I could not understand why. Two months later I had not concluded all the books, but I called him to begin the classes anyway.

During our first session, I told him that I was puzzled. "The three books you asked me to read sort of kind of have the same messages and teachings," I said.

"What is the common denominator?" he asked me.

"They all preach about the Oneness of God. And about peace and love," I answered. "The practices related to 'the Way of Life,' the last Religion, believed in all the other prophets. Abraham, Moses, Jesus, and Mohammed were recognized and acknowledged." I looked at the cleric and went on, "So why are we fighting each other? Why are we not allowed to interact or intermarry and so forth?"

His response surprised me, coming from a well-known and learned Muslim cleric in Tunisia. "It's all about the numbers!"

He said *numbers*? What numbers? None was wrong, but there was something about the "following" of a particular religion. What he meant was that there is sometimes too much emphasis on the number of people who convert to one religion, or on the number of followers of one religion, or on the number of areas that one book makes reference to a significant religious era that another did not, rather than focusing on the qualitative aspect of religion as teachings from the one God as a way of life.

Given how controversial discussions, opinions, and perceptions abound over what the different religions say and preach, I will focus on the thrust of my story, but affirm that I believe in *all three books* based on—first and foremost—The Oneness of God! The existence of the Prophets of the "Three Books" amongst other Prophets—Abraham, Prophet Moses, Prophet Jesus and Prophet Mohammed. This can be debatable. But that is the core for me. Having read so many self-help personal development and motivational books and watched so many videos on the same, I've tried and tested many of the spiritual tools and processes. I am amazed at how simple some of them were and how easy they were to get once I got the hang of it.

I started to develop strong intuitions, I was able to sense

energy dynamics, I could see "signs" in everything from sign posts in the streets to conversations that I overheard, to photos or email messages popping up. The more I became aware, the more I acknowledged and accepted that I was on the right track. I signed up for online webinars and courses of Neale Walsch and other spiritual gurus. My intuition grew stronger and stronger to the point that I could be having a telephone conversation with someone and sense whether something was right or not at the other end, either just by hearing their voice or sensing the energy dynamics.

It was during this time alone in Tunis, following a routine annual medical check in January 2015, that the mammogram revealed three lumps on my left breast and two on my right. The clinic in which I undertook the examination recommended I undergo further tests. The final results revealed that there were indeed tumours, all benign. Except for one. I decided immediately to have all the lumps, tumours, cysts, whatever they found in the tests and were unsure of, removed. I was not afraid, but I was not ready to take chances either.

One of the doctors in my organisation's medical centre referred me to a breast cancer specialist, the best in Tunisia. I called my mum and my husband, as I was alone in Tunis at the time, to give them the news. Mum's reaction was that the world was coming to an end. She was more worried than I was and was in tears.

I was actually so calm that the doctor recommended I get some sort of counselling therapy, as she felt I may be having delayed shock or be in denial. I was neither in denial nor was I having a delayed shock. I felt that I had gone through so many physical and emotional ordeals that I had reached a point whereby nothing could break me down any more.

In March 2015, I had surgery to remove the tumors on both breasts. The surgery itself was a painful experience and required a lot of adjustments. Following surgery, my daughter visited for a week and her company made a huge difference. I had turned down going through chemotherapy and agreed to opt for radiotherapy only if necessary. I decided against taking any form of medication and relied on my faith and my inner strength to see me through this process. With my husband in Dakar and no family members living close by to help, I had to handle this on my own. Perhaps I even preferred it that way.

I got my inspiration for the whole process from my maternal grandmother. She had breast cancer and carried this pain with her for seven years without telling anyone. The first time we knew about it was ten days before she died when she unusually did not get out of bed. When asked what was wrong with her, she told my mum she had malaria. The following day, my grandmother's maid called my mum and expressed concern that my grandmother's health was deteriorating and that she moaned and groaned the entire night before. Mum insisted and took my grandmother to the doctors. That's when we found out that my grandmother had been keeping this a secret from the entire family. She explained that if she had raised the alarm, everyone would make a fuss and would want to suggest she travel to the United Kingdom or Dakar to seek medical help, and that she just did not want to put anyone through any trouble, and besides, she didn't want anyone in her business and telling her what to do and what not to do. Ten days later, after precisely what she was running away from—the hustle and bustle and fuss—she died.

I felt the same way. My children were in the UK and were at university; my mother was still recovering a year after from my dad's passing and after going through six years of caring for her own cancer patient. I could not put my loved ones through this pressure, and besides, I did not want the hustle and bustle and fuss, or the sympathy.

Eight months after my first surgical operation, I started radiotherapy and further tests. Every part of my body was poked looking for signs and anything alien in my body. I lost my taste buds, I tired very easily, and often had pains thereafter. There were days when my immune system was low and I really could not do much for myself. Some days the pain was so bad, I could not even turn around on the bed or get out of bed. It was a battle between the cancer and myself.

I would often stand in front of the mirror and look myself in the mirror and say, "You want war? Bring it on; but this is one battle you will not win." I would wear bright clothes to boost my spirits. I continued with my work, travelling, taking on online coaching and leadership courses. Unless the pain was unbearable, I ignored the fact that it was there.

Family and friends who knew about the cancer made so much fuss that I had to make a deliberate effort to cut them off. I did not want to be reminded. Some suggested I take the soursop leaves, fruits and seeds; others suggested I take lots of ginger, and the list goes on. Some of my poor friends took it upon themselves to conduct online research on how to manage and minimise the growth of the cells. Everyone became a specialist on cancer.

I had a different therapy: to not dignify acknowledging its existence and declare psychological warfare on it. It worked for me. It meant I did not have to see myself as "the poor victim," that I did not have to feel sorry for myself, that I did not have to be afraid of so many "what ifs."

My lack of fear, and the faith and courage I garnered going through my medical process amazed my doctors, especially when I told them I was not afraid to die. I was at peace with myself, at peace with God, and at peace with everyone in my life and at peace with my relationship with God.

TAMING THE BEAST

I am naturally a very organised person. Organised to a fault, in fact. I was so organised when I travelled all the time, that I'd pack a week before my travels with a list of all the things that need to be in my suitcase. I would usually make two lists—one neatly placed in the suitcase and the other in my handbag to double check once I got to my destination. I kept a reflective diary, had a "to do list" and would plan family holidays months in advance. When we had family outings, I would bring along toilet wipes and medications for any disease that we may encounter on the way. I prepared meals, coolers all lined up. Check the petrol tanks, the tires checked and rechecked the weather, traffic jams, etc.

I would buy double of everything. One of my best friends once mentioned that sometimes she wonders whether I was actually born a twin and that my twin did not survive birth. When I asked her why, she said, "You always buy everything twice or double everything. Everything." I hadn't even noticed that I did that until she mentioned it. The fact of the matter is that I try to prepare for "just in case." Even today, I have a "just-in-case bag." I throw an umbrella in the just-in-case bag, a pair of flip-flops or flat shoes, just in case my shoes cut my feet on the way. I have two pairs of glasses, just in case one accidentally breaks. I have three mobiles, one just for back up with all the numbers (fortunately thanks to iCloud, that part of life has become less complicated).

As my awareness grows, I have come to realise that all of this "just-in-case" prep stuff and excessive planning weeks ahead has been a cover-up. A cover-up that I was a control freak. Not an aggressive one, though.

One of the biggest lessons for me in recognizing what a control freak I was happened with my eldest son when he was going off to the university for the first time. Aside from requesting to sign on the different dotted lines on the forms, I did and prepared everything, as well as communicated with the university. The boy was eighteen years old. I thought I was being the good, loving and caring mother. I told him what course he should enroll for, I went to the university with him for the new student intake, and asked all of the questions. I filled the forms about the rooms he should apply for. I spoke to Student Finance as if I were the student. I shopped for everything I thought he would need to settle in on campus. Just think of anything that one can possibly have at WH Smiths, Argos and Next; he got it all. We filled an entire seven-seater van to haul his stuff to university.

A year later, he called me one evening as I was driving home from work. "Mum," he started, "I am not sure I want to continue pursuing Computers Systems Engineering anymore. I would like to take on Electrical Engineering."

I was driving on the M40 and almost had an accident. I had to park on the nearest hard shoulder of the motorway, turn on the hazard lights, put up the windows and cry as if I had just been told I lost someone close. I cried for a good forty-five minutes. Finally, I dried my eyes and drove home. When I told my husband about the call, he was very casual about it and said, "If that is what he wants to do, then let him." I did not speak with my son for, I think, two months after that.

To say I had a big ego would be an understatement. I had told everyone that my son who is so good with computers was studying computer systems engineering at Canterbury University. Now what will the neighbors say? What will my family and friends say? That was all I could think of. Never once did I ask him whether he was having problems with the initial course or the teacher. No. Why should I? My ego was bruised because he was not living my dream. The same pathology I had defied when my parents decided on what I should pursue at college, how I should behave in the presence of visitors, was the same thing I was doing to my eldest son. How ironic.

Time passed by and although he was still staying at the university campus, he was not attending lectures. Today, eight years later, after attempts at two different universities, he decided it was not a path for him.

What did I learn from this lesson? I cannot push my son to live my life. What I know now is my role as a mother was to be a custodian. His path and life purpose is already determined and I may have contributed to setting him back a few years because of my interference. I fought my ego and had the courage to tell him how sorry I was for putting so much pressure on him because he was my eldest, amongst other things; that I had high hopes and plans for him which were not his plans, but mine. I asked for his forgiveness, gave him my blessings to get on with where his passion is and assured him that I will be around if he needed my advice and guidance, and that was about it. No more judgment, no more finger pointing. My love for him as a mother remains unconditional.

I took this lesson and applied the same to my other children. I know now when not to get involved in their lives. I set boundaries as their mother and let go, believing that the foundation I gave them during the early stages of their lives should be an indicator of whether I did my best to raise them. I love them all very dearly and am proud of each of them. I have come to accept and appreciate how diverse and different all four of them are. Today, they all live separately and independently.

I have grown older and wiser and have actually come to accept that "the sky is not going to fall down" if things happen the other way than I'd intended. I have learned to ask my husband and children to do things without being frantic. I still set all the clocks in the house fifteen minutes fast as well as my watch. I still make my shopping lists. I still have a vision board. But, I have learned to let go and let God take control.

I have learned to tame the beast—my ego—and this has been my greatest achievement. With time I have become very observant and aware of the ego voice inside of me. This is not my intuition. My intuition has over the years become so strong that if I wanted to do something or go somewhere but it doesn't feel right, I just don't do it. My father used to say that when you get to a certain age in your life you can do whatever you liked and get away with it and it does not matter what or how people felt. My dad's slogan was misdirected and out of context. My motto is now "If it doesn't feel right, I am not doing it" and so far I have no regrets given how much trust I have in my intuition.

Intuition and ego are indeed different, although, I sometimes have to be extra attentive so as to distinguish which one is trying to speak. When the ego chatter in my head keeps going on, I simply stand in front of a mirror, or if there is no mirror, I just say to it, "I know it is you and I do not wish to indulge in this conversation. I am not listening and will not listen to you." This works miracles for me. The thought disappears. And if another thought appears I repeat my words. I watch as a bystander and acknowledge the chattering and then say, "I am not going down that path with you," or, "Just stop it."

Similarly, I can actually say to myself, "I do not like the way I am feeling right now." I choose to change the feeling and can also choose to change the thought if it is not something I like. I practiced this for months and months and it has become an everyday part of living for me. I realise that the ego is not something one can get rid of, but one can actually diffuse its power.

When my husband and son joined me in Abidjan after a year of being separated while I was in Tunisia and they were in Dakar, I was excited that we were finally together again. I could not wait. As soon as I picked them up at the airport, I felt something was not right. I was not sure what it was, but I could feel some very strong negative energy.

A week later we were trying to rush the unfinished building

we had rented in a bid to expedite the construction process for moving into our new house in Abidjan. My husband went to the construction site to supervise the workers in the mornings and I went to work. This particular day was during the Holy month of Ramadan. I decided to take my lunch break and go join him at the construction site. He was not expecting me.

I took the flight of stairs and found him at the top of the balcony. He was on the phone, his tablet actually, without his headphones. I heard two women's voices talking and laughing on the other end. As I walked closer, he lifted his head and saw me. Our eyes locked. He froze for a few seconds. His face changed and became serious as he immediately started perspiring. When his senses came around, he switched off the phone.

"Who were they?" I asked.

"Ah, no one, just some of my friends' girlfriends." His perspiration became intense. It was humid.

"Why would you be sitting upstairs here during Ramadan, giggling and joking with your friends' girlfriends?" That did not sound right to me. "Who are they?"

"Oh, you don't know them."

"Let me see," I said as I walked closer to him.

By this time he was frantically trying to delete messages. I had tight knots in my stomach and my intuition snapped; I could tell this was not my ego. I insisted that I wanted to see, snatched the tablet from him, went back downstairs, got into my car and drove back to the office. I was trembling, but I did not cry or get angry. I was just very disappointed.

Then my ego jumped in and started the chattering: *All these years I have been working to provide for us, taking responsibility of his children and him. And now this? Other women? I don't deserve this!*

By the time I returned to the office and switched on the tablet, one of the girls had blocked him so I could not discover who she was. Through the search on his tablet, I came across some of their communication threads.

Unable to concentrate on work, I went home. My husband had also returned home from the construction site. When I asked him what this was all about, he explained everything. My head started to spin. This had been going on for three months. Every time he went to The Gambia from Dakar with excuses to sort things out, they would hook up. He was spending the money I sent him for the upkeep of the house on these girls. And he was using my car to drive them around.

His excuse was that I was in Tunis. He was lonely and vulnerable.

I was equally lonely. I was not enjoying being alone in Tunis. It later dawned on me that the time I was having surgery to remove the cancerous tumors in my breasts was precisely the time he was in Gambia having a good time, leaving our nine-year-old son in Dakar with the maid.

My ego was doing gymnastics in my head.

I have been living alone under extremely difficult circumstances particularly with my health, equally lonely, running four homes single-handedly with my children scattered in the USA, the UK, and Senegal, and my mum still mourning the death of my dad. In the meantime, my husband was cheating on me?

After he finished explaining, I started to think about the recent 90-day "Letting Go and Forgiveness" workshop I had just undergone with Iyanla and Inner Visions. I thought of the conversations I'd had with my 85-year-old Islamic cleric. I thought of the 7-day mental diet I'd been through. I was determined this must be a test by the universe to ascertain how ready I actually was to "let go." I felt I was being tested to ascertain my level of commitment—how far I wanted to go to be good, feel good, see good, do good and say good. The one year that I had been alone embarking on my spiritual journey, I had grown, matured, become wiser and this was the ultimate test.

Having gone through all this flashback, I garnered the courage to take a few deep breaths, inhale again and exhale three times. He was sitting there on the bed next to me, fiddling with his hands but unable to look me in the eye.

"You know what?" I said finally. "I forgive you. I forgive you for myself. I forgive you because I want to be at peace with myself. I forgive you in order to remain sane. I forgive you because I do not want to carry this excess baggage that has nothing to do with me."

This was not my problem. This was his problem. To be honest, I actually felt very light after that short and to the point conversation. I was still shocked. There was no drama. I did not cry, which was very unlike me. He was not expecting that reaction from me. He sat there numb and unable to move. Until I told him he could get up and go back to the living room. He just sat there frozen and would not move until I walked out of the room and left him sitting on the bed alone. After a while, he joined me in the living room and I had moved on with getting on with what I was doing that evening.

My ego had shifted from its gymnastics to monkey dancing around my thoughts. I prayed for the girls he'd been fooling around with. I spoke aloud that I forgave them. I prayed to God to erase the messages I had seen off my mind. I actually gave thanks for the lesson I learnt about my husband and his extra marital affairs. I gave thanks for reacting in a mature way, that when he chose to act as low as he did my response was more dignified, and that I had the ability to rise above it. Not that I will ever forget the incident, but I sincerely found it in my heart to forgive him.

What I know now is that I have no control over what he does or how he does what he does, but I can choose to react differently to whatever he does. That is what I do have control over: my reaction.

My husband and I have now both grown in this process and are able to feel each other's energy dynamics when it is in the environment. We are comfortable to say to each other, "I do not feel comfortable with the mood and energy around us right now," and we are able to work on it. Similarly, we have become contented in accepting, acknowledging and appreciating when something does not feel right.

I have thrown in the towel to the need to be right all the time. To being controlling about how everything should be. I feel happier. I feel at peace. Letting go of that leftover baggage was the best thing I could do for myself and for my family. I feel light. I am a lot happier and a lot closer with my husband and children now.

When the ego pops in every now and again, I just observe, smile and say, "We are not going down that path today."

IN LOVE WITH GRATITUDE

I write everything down, from shopping lists to vision boards, just anything. There's one little thing that I kept doing to my lists and never thought anything of it. When going through my lists, as I always do, I will tick the end of the item, write *received with thanks* and then date it. It is just a crazy habit I have developed.

Living in the Ivory Coast now, I say thank you to my chef every day as I leave the dinner table. I thank the housekeeper and the night watchman for performing their daily duties every evening. I say thank you to my driver every time he drops me off at the office or at home. When I drive myself and find a perfect parking spot, I will say thank you. Whenever I receive a blessing, I look upwards and just say, "God, you got me on this one. It was a pleasant and unexpected surprise. Thank you." I say thank you for anything. I do not wait until it is time for prayers; it is just second nature to me now.

What I didn't know was that this gratitude was the key to unlocking doors for me. As a child and teen girl, I was grateful to be a part of a family with so much and I wanted to share our family's bounty with those less fortunate, just like Aunty Mama did. I was punished for it then, but now as an adult, after restoration and healing, I am free to celebrate in my gratitude. A revelation became clear to me—the more I expressed gratitude, the more I received a flow of abundance coming my way from all angles. I feel like I found "*the* secret." Thank you, thank you, thank you has become my "open sesame" to unlock the doors of abundance to the universe.

Earlier this summer, I had promised the family that we would start off our summer vacation for our son Taff's graduation in the USA and then we would all fly together to the UK for our daughter Katty's graduation. I was waiting for my annual leave travel benefit funds in time to purchase the air tickets for the entire family. In the meantime, I used available resources to buy tickets for my husband and youngest son for the first leg of the trip to the USA. Once in the USA I checked my online banking statement three times a day to see if the funds had arrived yet, to no avail.

Then some strange miraculous magic happened. I went online on payday to check once again. There were no home leave funds transferred, but somehow they had accidentally double paid me my salary. *How could that have happened?* My organization, particularly the finance department, was so stringent. How could they have mistakenly paid me my salary twice? I knew and felt Divine intervention had my back. I looked up and said, "You truly are the Alpha and the Omega; the greatest I AM and I love you dearly. Thank you, thank you, thank you.

We spent the money, had the vacation, and three months later the finance department contacted me to inform me they had made a mistake and double paid my salary in error. I replied, yes, I know. By this time the home leave funds had been transferred. I used part of that money and repaid the bank.

I knew deep down in my heart that someone up there loves me and I felt the love. These little miracles—as I always love to call them—keep happening whenever obstacles come up. A similar thing happened with my son's university fees in the USA. I needed to have a bank account statement reflecting the expected amount of tuition fees for him to get accepted at university. Where was I going to find this money? We had just come from his and his sister's graduations, followed by holidays as a family, and I had spent every dime I had.

As God would have it, I was alerted that there remained an

excess in an education grant that I had paid for the year before. They needed to repay me the difference. *Two financial miracles in one month?* I went inside my bathroom, sat on the floor, and sobbed. I said "thank you!" so many times that the phrase stuck in my head the whole day and throughout the night.

I fell in love with gratitude—the secret—because the more I said thank you, the more I received without even knowing how it happened, where it came from, or when it manifested.

I made a decision to develop a daily mantra and daily affirmation. I say these words first thing in the morning before I get out of bed. Most times I say them the moment I am conscious, even without opening my eyes. I do the same thing at bedtime as I lie on the bed and close my eyes to sleep. These recitations are a mix of prayers I learnt as a little girl at the Methodist primary school and the normal standard daily recitation prayers of both Muslim and Christian in Arabic and in English.

This habit is engrained as part of my daily life and being. It has become such a regular practice that I cannot sleep or get out of bed without reciting them, just like the daily five times a day prayers. In addition, when I am on board an airplane, I do the same as soon as it is on the runway about to take off and just when the plane is about to land. The feeling one gets when they miss out on praying, that strange urge or feeling, a voice reminding you that you have not prayed—that is what this practice has become to me.

My daily mantra and affirmation begins with the following. I am sure many will be familiar with this simple prayer that has been taught to children at a young age:

Thank you, Thank you, Thank you.
Thank you, Thank you, Thank you.
Thank you, Thank you, Thank you.
Thank you, God, for the world so sweet.
Thank you, God, for the food we eat.
Thank you, God, for the birds that sing.
Thank you, God, for everything.
Amen.

After this simple prayer, I launch into a series of mantras, affirmations, and prayers. (See My Daily Mantras and Affirmations at the back of the book.) I also recite an additional daily prayer every morning, committing my soul to God and submitting to his plans for the day. I will never leave my house or hotel room or wherever I am in the morning without seeking for guidance for the day, and it works for me like magic. These repeated practices have been the secret of my abundance and success in everything I do or say.

Months after learning of my husband's affairs, I wrote a letter to God and asked him about my husband cheating on me and why I had to go through this process. I felt I was a good wife, a good mother, and a good daughter. Everything I have was for my family. What was he trying to teach me through this? I asked him to respond through me, through the same pen that I used to write the letter to him. He responded, but in a different way than I'd requested. The experience was unreal.

The response started blurting, not through the pen, but out of my mouth. I was talking with my husband in our hotel room in Giza, next to the Pyramids in Cairo, at 3am one morning, when the words started flowing. I don't know what happened but the words and sound did not even sound like my voice. I spoke as if I were reading from a piece of paper or a book, the words squabbling out of my mouth. My husband lay quietly and listened as I spoke and blurted out the response, unrehearsed and unexpected:

"Did I not make you so strong and independent that you do not have to rely on anyone but your strength, courage and wisdom to financially take care of your husband, parents, and children and even others?

Did I not at your tender age of thirty call upon you to the Holy City with your own finances and no support from anyone, at a time when women were not allowed to perform the Holy Pilgrimage alone without a male relative accompanying them?

Did I not make you strong to be able to withhold all the disappointments and betrayals and still come out of it forgiving and embracing?

Did I not choose you amongst many to go where many hath not gone and explored so much; where many hath not seen?

Did I not increase your faith that you fear not even death or pain?

Have I not increased your connection to your soul that you have become best friends with your intuition; so strong that you worry not?

Have I not demonstrated to you that because you trusted me so much and genuinely that when you thought it was impossible to pay university fees for four of your responsibilities at the same time in one month, when you were under pressure and still had to attend two graduations across two continents in the same month with your family, when all possibilities proved futile, and yes you did?

Have you not noticed that I have been distancing you from the public not because there may be negative influences but because you have committed to be open to the possibilities of abundance and gratitude, that you yearn to use what you have today gained to help heal souls; thus the universe needed to protect you?

Have I not given you the power of a man to be present during your father's burial when you were in another country and called upon by men in your community to stand before the corpse of your father to pray for him in the privacy of his bedroom prior to his burial when in your tradition this is not allowed for women?

Have I not given you the power to own properties in other countries other than your own when you felt that all the money that you have you have invested in your parents, your husband and children and worried about your future after retirement?

Have I not elevated you to positions that have been designated for men and above all obstacles, placed you there because I believed in you?

Then why do you question the lessons I continue to instill onto you?"

Assured I was finished, my husband stared at me, stunned and speechless, unable to say a word. Even I was speechless after that encounter. He finally drifted back to sleep, but I was too shocked to sleep. I lay beside him with my eyes closed and stayed awake all night, afraid to open my eyes in case I saw something in the room I should not see.

The next day after this 3am encounter, the hotel management called us and asked whether we were ready to move to another room. We were checked in at the Mena Oberoi Hotel, right next to the Giza Pyramids in Egypt.

Not understanding what the receptionist was trying to say, I said over the phone, "No need to clean the room today. We will be staying indoors."

"No," he said, "You have been upgraded to one of the newly refurbished rooms because there was a problem with the shower in your room."

Byes went to check the shower. There was nothing wrong with it.

The hotel clerk told us to get ready to move. Fifteen minutes later hotel staff came and jumbled up all our stuff. We were really not prepared for this. They shuttled us and all of our things to the other side of the hotel closer to the pyramids.

When my husband and I walked into the room, we were stunned. Why the upgrade? Surely, we definitely could not afford this room. Baskets and baskets of fruits with local Egyptian pastries were being sent to our room. The suite, the view, the service. Only someone "up there" could continue to be sending us his love.

I was on an official mission and had decided to bring my husband along so he could enjoy a break whilst I was busy with my meetings. This trip turned into so much more. After our special time at the Mena Oberoi Hotel in Egypt, we agreed to continue to express our love and appreciation for each other, to be more open to each other about our feelings and our plans of what we would do to spend more quality time together. We call it "the Mena Declaration."

IT IS MY DESIRE

Once upon a time, I was a bubbly person who was everywhere, anywhere. And with everybody I was a people pleaser. I got a high from pleasing people. I am generally a very loving, kind-hearted, extroverted, helpful, people pleaser. What I have discovered is that as one ages or matures, less is more. The growth process of transformation has made me more of an introvert now. I have become so confident in myself and so comfortable with myself that sometimes I wonder where it all came from.

These days I am also more private than I used to be. My career requires extensive traveling. Giving keynote addresses. Meeting with Ministers. Meeting with Heads of State, High-level dignitaries. It requires being interviewed on television, sitting on global advisory boards, etc. After these public engagements, I enjoy my alone time and my own company. In fact, I love my me time.

As I grow older and mature, the force of gravity, or nature, has determined the people who cross my path for a reason, others for a season, and others for a lifetime. I have learnt that every person who crosses my path has a lesson to teach me and that it is for me to figure out what that lesson is. For those who dropped off on the way, I send them love; I have no malice, no hard feelings, no anger or no regrets. Perhaps we just no longer align with one another and that is okay. I have learnt that by age fifty you start shedding off what does not resonate with you anymore.

Sometimes I say to myself, if only I knew then what I know now, I would have done a lot of things differently. But then . . . that would not have been how it should be. I had to go through all of these processes, this entire journey, to arrive at where I am now. I have been particularly lucky and blessed to have a beautiful family. A loving and caring husband. Wonderful children, great love and friendship with my mum and siblings. I have been fortunate finding jobs that I enjoy and jobs that resonate with my passion. Some more passionate than others. However, I believe that each job prepared me for the next.

When these young African girls look up to me and say, "We want to be like you when we grow up," I say to them, "Each with his or her own journey." They will each have to go through their own pathways to arrive at their destination, to find themselves and their purpose in life.

I have learnt that there is no such thing as right or wrong. We cannot tell people to stop doing things one way or the other when it is in their pathology, when this is how they grew up or were raised to be.

I believe our roles as spirits is to help each other find our-selves. I benefitted from having a beautiful soul, lots of blessings particularly from my parents and husband, belief and prayers, and I still do, but they alone could not help me learn who I truly am. I still look up to those who found themselves and believed in their inner self to be what they had to be today. They have my admiration, but they do not determine my identity. I can only be me.

I was inspired by listening to Dr. Wayne Dyer when he explained in one of his lectures about how when we are in our mother's womb without any care of wondering how we eat, breathe, survive, without thinking of what makes this all happen and who makes this all happen, yet we trust this source to take care of all that needs to be taken care of inside our mother's womb. As soon as the umbilical cord is cut, sep-arating us from the Source, we are labeled. After our excited parents thank God for our safe arrival, they then take it from there, and that's where the labeling starts: you are a boy or a

girl; a Muslim, Christian or Jew. You have a name. You are
black or white. You are of this nationality; you belong to this
group; and the list goes on. But this is not who we are. This
label does not represent our soul.

The numbers of followers amongst organised religions are a
reflection and indication that there are a lot of people in Africa,
and the world at large, yearning to connect with God or their
Higher self. They don't realise that they do not need to go
anywhere, to anyone, but to learn to look inward.

I keep asking myself, "How can I help people to find the
answer they seek inside of them?"

In my personal and professional journey, I come across so
many troubled youths: some lost; some misunderstood; some
stuck, bitter and angry with everyone including themselves;
some depressed and don't know how to start to untangle themselves. Many have no confidence in themselves. The need for
healing, especially in my continent and even more so in my
country of origin, The Gambia, is imminent. Unfortunately
most do not know how to go about or how to start the process of personal growth. The knowledge required to achieve
personal, professional and spiritual growth is not often taught
in schools, in colleges, in universities, and sometimes not at
the home front or within our societies.

My mission as an African woman is to inspire people to
discover their own pathways. I want to help motivate them
to aspire to achieve their desired dreams and wishes through
ways in which I couldn't understand when I was growing up.
As I continue to grow and new discoveries emerge to help
me align with my life purpose, it is my desire to coach young
women and girls, and young boys as well, to help them discover
and align with their life purpose. It is my desire to help them
embrace the positive implications of forgiving, trusting again,
managing their thoughts, their minds, and growing. It is my
desire through mentoring and coaching to help them learn
how to live a life of gratitude that brings peace and inspiration,
and how to attract the abundance that already awaits them.

Coaching, a partnership between two individuals, is still a

new concept in the African context. It is my desire to coach others to grow in her or his personal, professional and spiritual growth. In so doing, I hope to bring new growth and knowledge to my home country and continent as well, just like my father and other young ambitious Gambian university graduates did before me many years earlier.

I have asked myself, "Who am I to coach others? What gives me the right and authority to qualify and coach others?" At first, I became uncomfortable at the thought of these questions. Then it dawned on me that I have actually been coaching people informally without even realizing it. Over the years I have mentored members of my families, friends, peers and many others from different societies. I have acquired a wealth of wisdom through life's lessons on my own personal, professional and spiritual journey, resulting in embarking on a coaching course and becoming a Certified Life and Spiritual Coach. In the process of continuing to grow in all aspects of my life through sharing my stories and making my own humble, positive and meaningful contribution in the lives of others, I continue to connect to my soul and fulfilling my purpose. This is what I want to spend the rest of my next fifty years doing and I believe that the universe is open to guide me through this process.

It is for this reason that I decided to share through my memoirs the stories of the lessons and blessings of my personal and professional journey as well as the stories of how I found my purpose. It is my hope that others may benefit and find inspiration from these stories that will in turn motivate them to find the pathways to achieve their purpose in life.

So for me, at fifty, married with four children and a decent job, I have ticked all my boxes. In terms of taking responsibilities towards my dad until he passed away, my mum, my husband, my children, and other young girls and boys inspired to aspire, I have earned myself the privilege to be who I am—Oley Dibba-Wadda.

EPILOGUE

After several consultations with my doctor, face-to-face visits and so many tests, I made the bold decision to opt for a double mastectomy. My daughter, Katty, then suggested that it would make sense to have reconstruction, if possible. She defended that as a public figure, it will affect the way I see myself and the way I dressed. She advised that irrespective of how strong I was, there will come a time that my self-esteem would be affected if I had to go about my business with a flat chest, as she would put it: "competing with Dad."

My doctor agreed it was the right choice, and on 1 December 2016, I had a five-hour double mastectomy and reconstruction surgical operation. Despite the excruciating pain after surgery I am happy I made the decision and grateful everything went smoothly.

As the healing process continues, I am beginning to feel less anxious of how life will be with these new objects in my body. Counselling and physiotherapy have proved very helpful in my recovery process. My faith and spiritual journey have also helped me, making me more accepting of the occurrences in my life. I believe that over time I will be able to share my story with so many others who are struggling in this journey.

I am fortunate to have my mother, my husband, my children and my siblings for the daily support and encouragement I receive from them. My friends and colleagues have been very supportive and understanding too. I feel the love that surrounds me and I am blessed to have all these people in my life who care so much about my health and well-being.

My mother with whom I talk about anything under the sun is my best friend, my guide, my anchor and my closest ally. We have become dependent on each other's company. Even though we live in different countries, we talk every week, sometimes three to four times in a week, and our conversations can go on for more than an hour about anything and everything.

My only daughter, Katty, is a young lady who knows what she wants and how to get it. She has vision, is focused, an extrovert, adventurous, open-minded and a go-getter. Sometimes I suspect she inherited the dynamism of my great-grand-aunt Aunty Mama. But what I do know is that with or without our nudge, she already has her life all sourced out. As of this writing, Katty has started her Master's Degree in Drug Design at the University of Bath in the United Kingdom.

My boys and I have a different relationship. The eldest, Omar, is now married. His wife, Mariam, equally shares similar DNA as my daughter and myself, knowing what we want and going for it. "But I ain't budging and I ain't involving." Mariam is another blessing and addition to the family, and is like a daughter to me, more than just a daughter-in-law. She continues to help Omar mature, grow and take on adult responsibilities. Omar and I will always have diverse perspectives about anything and everything. He enjoys, and as I always tell him, is addicted to our debates, something he thrives on being philosophical about. However, our love and bond is special; he calls it "tough love." Mustapha, like Omar, also loves debates and to psychoanalyze, and has started his undergraduate studies at Bethel University in Tennessee in Southern United States. Given that our youngest son, Samsu, is his dad's baby, Mustapha remains *my* baby (albeit nineteen years of age). Samsu, now eleven years old and his dad's best friend, attends the International Community School of Abidjan (ICSA).

I learnt the hard way of weaning myself off of my children to provide them with the space to grow. It was a tough experience. I now appreciate that I am only a custodian and at this stage of their lives, they should pretty much be able to find their bearings without me interfering.

Over the years my husband has matured with age and has started to pamper me, like preparing breakfast in bed and making morning coffee for me. Today he has become my doctor, my nurse, the big brother I never had and my friend. He is my confidant, my adviser and the love of my life. In spite of the challenges we faced in our marriage during the early years, we became stronger together, growing old and gracefully aging together, particularly as the kids have left the nest. It is surprising for someone who was never home as a young family man during the early days of our marriage, how now one literally has to drag him to get him out of the house. He is a loving husband and a great father. In spite of all the rough patches Byes and I have gone through together in our marriage, today we serve as role models to many young couples. I will not change him for all the diamonds of the world.

I am grateful to have my mother, my husband, and my children around me. I could not ask for more.

Thank you, Thank you, Thank you.
Thank you, Thank you, Thank you.
Thank you, Thank you, Thank you.
Thank you, God, for the world so sweet.
Thank you, God, for the food we eat.
Thank you, God, for the birds that sing.
Thank you, God, for everything.
Amen.

This is followed by:

O God my Heavenly Father, I thank you for my life, I thank
you for my family and I thank you for my friends.
Father, I thank you for my joy, I thank you for my peace, I
thank you for my love and I thank you for my happiness.
I thank you, Father, for receiving everything good and I thank
you, Father, for receiving everything positive.
Father, I thank you for putting me on the same frequency as
Divine Intervention.
I thank you, Father, for putting me in control of my subconscious
and I thank you, Father, for providing me with the skills and
knowledge to restore and resurrect my soul.
I thank you, Father, for my abundance.
Father, I thank you for my success.
I thank you for my career.
I thank you for my skills and knowledge.
I thank you for my confidence.
I thank you for my ambition and I thank you for my riches.
I thank you, Father, for my health. I thank you for my wealth
and I thank you for my wisdom.
I thank you, Father, for my compassion.
Father, I thank you for my kind heart.
I thank you for my generosity.
I thank you for my kindness.
I thank you for my gentleness.
I thank you for my tolerance.

I thank you for my patience and I thank you for my humility.
I thank you, Father, for my commitment.
I thank you for my determination; I thank you for my persever-
ance.
Father, I thank you for my enthusiasm.
I thank you for my courage and I thank you for my positivity.
I thank you, Father, for my inspiration.
I thank you for my motivation.
I thank you for my gratitude and I thank you for my blessings.
I thank you, Father, for all that I am and for all that I have.
Thank you! Thank you! Thank you!

This is followed by the mother of all secrets—my "I AM" mantra.

Because of this, Father, I AM joy. I AM peace. I AM love. I AM happy. I AM contented. I AM satisfied. I AM grateful. I AM blessed. I AM compassionate. I AM kindhearted. I AM gentle. I AM understanding. I AM tolerant, I AM patient, I AM humble, I AM committed, I AM determined, I AM perseverance, I AM enthusiastic, I AM courageous, I AM positive, I AM beautiful on the inside, I AM beautiful on the outside, I AM receiving everything good and I AM receiving everything positive. I AM on the same frequency as Divine Intervention, I AM in control of my subconscious, I have the skills and knowledge to restore and resurrect my soul. I AM abundant. I AM successful. I AM skillful. I AM rich. I AM healthy. I AM wealthy. I AM wise. I AM that, I AM. I AM that, I AM. I AM that, I AM. Thank you. Thank you. Thank you; Thank you, Thank you, Thank you; Thank you, Thank you, Thank you!

Followed by:

The Lord is my shepherd; I shall not want. He maketh me to lie down in green pastures. He leadeth me beside the still waters. He restoreth my soul. He leadeth me in the paths of righteousness, for his namesake. Yea, though I walk through the valley of the shadows of death, I will fear no evil. For thou art with me. Thy rod and thy staff, they comfort me. Thou preparest a table before me in the presence of mine enemies. Thou anointeth my head with oil, my cup runneth over. Surely goodness and mercy shall follow me all the days of my life. And I will dwell in the house of the Lord, forever. Amen.

Followed by:

Our Father, who art in Heaven. Hallowed be Thy name. Thy Kingdom come. Thy will be done on earth as it is in Heaven. Give us this day our daily bread. And forgive us our trespasses. As we forgive those who trespass against us. And lead us not into temptation. But deliver us from evil. For Thine is the Kingdom. The Power and the Glory. Forever and ever. Amen.

Followed by:

Salawat Al-Fatih *(when opening prayers) Allahumma salli ' wa sallim was baarik ala Sayyidina Muhammadil, nil-fatihi lima Ughliqa wal khatimi lima sabaqa wan-naa-siril-haqqi, bil-haqqi wal-hadi ila Sirati-kal-mustaqima sal-lal-lahu 'alayhi, wa 'ala alihi wa-ashaabihi haqqa qadrihi wa-miq-da rihil-'azim.*

Meaning: "O Allah! May Thy grace, peace and bless-ings rest on Muhammad, our Master, who opens that which is closed, and closes that which is preceded, who helps truth with truth, and who guided mankind to Thy straight path. May blessings of Allah be on him and his Family and Companions as according to his exalted position befitting his merit and his high rank."

Surah Al-Fatiha (1) (The Opening) – Recite once—bismillaahir rahmaanir raheem. alhamdu lillaahi rabbil 'aalameen. ar-rahmaanir-raheem. maaliki yawmid-deen. iyyaaka na'budu wa lyyaaka nasta'een. ihdinas-sir-aatal-mustaqeem. siraatal-lazeena an'amta 'alaihim ghay-ril-maghdoobi 'alaihim wa lad-daaalleen

Meaning: In the name of Allah, Most Gracious, Most Merciful. Praise be to Allah, the Cherisher and Sustainer of the worlds; Most Gracious, Most Merciful; Master of the Day of Judgment. Thee do we worship, and Thine aid we seek. Show us the straight way. The way of those on whom Thou hast bestowed Thy Grace, those whose (portion) is not wrath, and who go not astray.

Surah Al-Falaq (113)—(The Dawn) – Recite once— Bismillaahir Rahmaanir Raheem. Qul a'uzoo bi rab-bil-falaq. Min sharri ma khalaq. Wa min sharri ghasiqin iza waqab. Wa min sharrin-naffaa-thaati fil 'uqad. Wa min shar ri haasidin iza hasad.

Meaning: I seek refuge with the Lord of the Dawn. From the mischief of created things; From the mischief of Darkness as it overspreads; From the mischief of those who practise secret arts; And from the mischief of the envious one as he practises envy.

Surah An-Nas (114) (The Men) – Recite once— Bismillaahir Rahmaanir Raheem. Qul a'uzu birabbin naas. Malikin naas. Ilaahin naas. Min sharril was waasil khannaas. Al lazee yuwas wisu fee sudoorin naas. Minal jinnati wan naas.

Meaning: I seek refuge with the Lord and Cherisher of Mankind. The King (or Ruler) of Mankind. The Allah (for judge) of Mankind,- From the mischief of the Whisperer (of Evil), who withdraws (after his whisper),- (The same) who whispers into the hearts of Mankind,- Among Jinns and among men.

Surah Al-Ikhlas (112)—(The Unity)—Recite once— Bismillaahir Rahmaanir Raheem Qul huwal laahu ahad. Allah hus-samad. Lam yalid wa lam yoolad. Wa lam yakul-lahu kufuwan ahad.

Meaning: He is Allah, the One and Only;. Allah, the Eternal, Absolute. He begetteth not, nor is He begotten. And there is none like unto Him.

Ayatul Kursi—Recite five times—Bismillaahir Rahmaanir Raheem—Allahu laaa ilaaha illaa huwal haiyul qai-yoom; laa taakhuzuhoo sinatunw wa laa nawm; lahoo maa fissamaawaati wa maa fil ard; man zallazee yashfa'u indahooo illaa be iznih; ya'lamu maa baina aideehim wa maa khalfahum; wa laa yuheetoona beshai 'immin 'ilmihee illa be maa shaaaa; wasi'a kursiyyuhus samaa waati wal arda wa la ya'ooduho hifzuhumaa; wa huwal aliyyul 'azeem.

Meaning: "Allah! There is no god but He—the Living, The Self-subsisting, Eternal. No slumber can seize Him Nor Sleep. His are all things In the heavens and on earth. Who is there can intercede In His presence except As he permitteth? He knoweth What (appeareth to His creatures As) Before or After or Behind them. Nor shall they compass Aught of his knowledge Except as He willeth. His throne doth extend Over the heavens And on earth, and He feeleth No fatigue in guarding And preserving them, For He is the Most High. The Supreme (in glory)."

Salawat Al-Fatih (when closing prayers) Allahumma salli ' wa sallim was baarik ala Sayyidina Muhammadil, nil-fatihi lima Ughliqa wal khatimi lima sabaqa wannaa-siril-haqqi, bil-haqqi wal-hadi ila Sirati-kal-mustaqima sal-lal-lahu 'alayhi, wa 'ala alihi wa-ashaabihi haqqa qadrihi wa-miq-da rihil-'azim.

Meaning: "O Allah! May Thy grace, peace and blessings rest on Muhammad, our Master, who opens that which is closed, and closes that which is preceded, who helps truth with truth, and who guided mankind to Thy straight path. May blessings of Allah be on him and his Family and Companions as according to his exalted position befitting his merit and his high rank."

MORNING RECITATION:

In addition, every morning after saying the above, I would then say the following:

"O God my Heavenly Father, Holy Spirit, Divine Intervention, Divine Mercy, My Soul, My Guide, My Source, My All. Good morning.

What is your agenda for me today?

What is it you will want me to do today and how will you want me to do this?

Show me the way, O Lord, Guide me, O Lord. Be with me, O Lord. Use Me, O Lord.

I surrender my Soul and My Body to you. I trust in you. I believe in you. I love you.

Use me, Father, use me. Take control.

Manifest your power over me. And let your will be done.

Amen and thank you.

ACKNOWLEDGMENTS

Aunty Mama, I continue to be inspired and drawn to your way of giving and helping those less fortunate. Women generations after you have picked up some of your traits; your influence rubbed off on Mum, my daughter, Katty, and myself.

To Mum (my rock) and Dad, everything I saw and learned under your wing has helped shape the woman I have become today. Thank you for the blessings.

My dear Byes, my pillar, thank you for the love, for the lessons and for the blessings.

To my children, Omar, Katty, Mustapha and Samsudeen, you continue to be the wind beneath my sails and my reason for being. My daughter-in-law, Mariam, thank you for your meaningful and constructive contribution to the memoir and my visionary ideas.

My dear siblings, Penda, Omey, and Lu. Thank you for crossing my path for the first half of my lifetime.

And to my family, friends, colleagues, role models and mentors, thank you for crossing my path for a reason and a season.

Special thanks to my editor, Kathy Groom. This book would not have been what it is today without you helping me bring it to life. The first time we connected, I knew in my heart that we were in for the long haul together, to make this project a success.

To my coach, Vivien Snape, yes indeed, I have value and I AM valuable. Your continued guidance and support make it possible for me to leap in spite of the fears.

ABOUT THE AUTHOR

Oley Dibba-Wadda is a strategic analyst and expert in international development policy and programming, particularly on education and gender equality in Africa. She is a mentor, a motivational speaker and a Certified Life and Spiritual Coach. She has lead multicultural and multidisciplinary Pan African development organisations and is the current Executive Secretary of the Association for the Development of Education in Africa (ADEA) hosted by the African Development Bank (AfDB). Prior, Oley was the Executive Director of Femmes Africa Solidarité (FAS) working on women, peace and security in Africa as well as the Forum for African Women Educationalists (FAWE) working on girls' education in 34 countries across Sub-Saharan Africa. Similarly, she worked with Oxfam GB in the UK as Global Programme and Policy Adviser and has held senior management and advisory roles such as Project Manager, Country Director and Regional Co-ordinator in other international organisations including Commonwealth Education Fund, Concern Universal and the European Development Fund. Oley has raised and managed multi-million US$ budgets through multilateral and bilateral cooperation agencies, foundations, governments and private individuals and successfully cultivated and nurtured strategic partnerships. Oley sits on several Advisory Boards and was a Global Ambassador for 10X10 and Concern Universal—she was also Chair of the Board of Trustees for Concern Universal. She has been invited to speak as panelist, keynote and guest speakers on numerous high level international forums globally. These include the Commonwealth Head's of Government Summit (CHOGAM) in Perth, Australia, The World Bank Gender and Education Colloquium in Washington amongst others.

LIFE PHILOSOPHY

Oley's well known quote towards her purpose and Life journey reads:

> "My Life is to give and share all that I AM and all that I have to humankind. I get my inspiration from the longing for love; the search for knowledge; gratitude for all that I AM and compassion for the living—This is My Life"

PERSONAL

Oley Dibba-Wadda is of Gambian origin and born in Oxford, United Kingdom. She is the eldest amongst 4 siblings and married and has one daughter and three sons.

EDUCATION

Oley Dibba-Wadda is a Doctoral Candidate and has a M.A. in Gender Analysis in Development from the University of East Anglia (UK), etc . . .

She is a certified Life and Spiritual Coach and Motivational Speaker

PRIZES & AWARDS

Oley is the first woman to head the Pan African institution – the Association for the Development of Education in Africa ADEA and was awarded "Inspiring Woman of Excellence" in The Gambia in 2012; and "Women Leadership Award" in Mauritius in 2013

READING LIST

Biographies and Autobiographies of well-known global leaders such as Nelson Mandella; Mahatma Ghandi; Au Sang su chi, President Bill Clinton, President Barack Obama as well as inspirational and self-help motivational books of spiritual gurus such as Iyanla Vanzant, Wayne Dyer, Deepack Chopra, Eckhart Tolie, Neal Walsh, Maya Angelo, Robin Sharma, Elizabeth Gilbert, Gary Zukav, Jill Bolte Taylor, Michael Samuels, Vic,

Johnson, Gregg Braden, Marian Williamson, Paulo Coelho, Patricia Gulley, David Hamilton, Andrea Gardner, Robert Collier, Kelly Wallace, Genevive Behrend, Rick Warren, Rhonda Byron, Sadhguru.

Oley has participated in specialized Self Development and motivational courses such as Fern Goin and Iyanla Vanzant.

FAVOURITE PAST-TIME

Oley indulges her weekends in either reading motivational books from her kindle or listening and watching online motivational programmes such as Oprah's Life Classes, Super Soul Sunday, Iyanla Fix my Life, Sadhguru, Deepak Chopra amongst others.

INTERNATIONAL ENGAGEMENTS

Oley sits on several Advisory Boards and was a Global Ambassador for 10X10 and Concern Universal—she was also Chair of the Board of Trustees for Concern Universal. She has been invited to speak as panelist, keynote and guest speakers on numerous high level international forums globally. These include the Commonwealth Heads of Government Summit (CHOGAM) in Perth, Australia, The World Bank Gender and Education Colloquium in Washington amongst others.

Oley has travelled the length and breadth of the Global serving as keynote speaker, motivational speaker, special guest speaker, and panelist on education, girls education, gender and women's rights in Africa.   She is a mentor to several young African women and men to facilitate and support them in aspiring to achieve academic, professional and personal excellence in their life and career paths by providing financial support towards their education as well as using her influence to place them as interns and young professional programmes in international development organizations.

Dad graduating from Oxford

Mum and Dad's wedding photo in London, September 9, 1966

Family compound in Fajara The Gambia

The family compound in later years

Great great grandfather, Jean Carayol

My maternal grandfather, Ernest Carayol

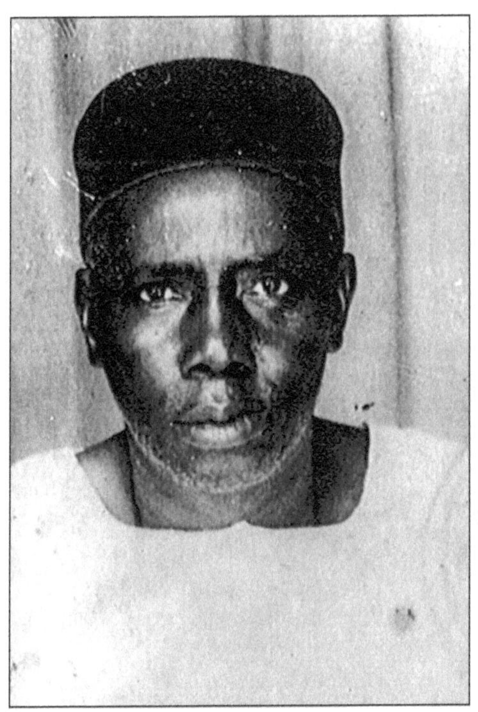

My paternal grandfather, Babou Dibba

Aunty Mama in a traditional Senegambia outfit

Mum and her mum at our home compound in the early years, the late 1970s

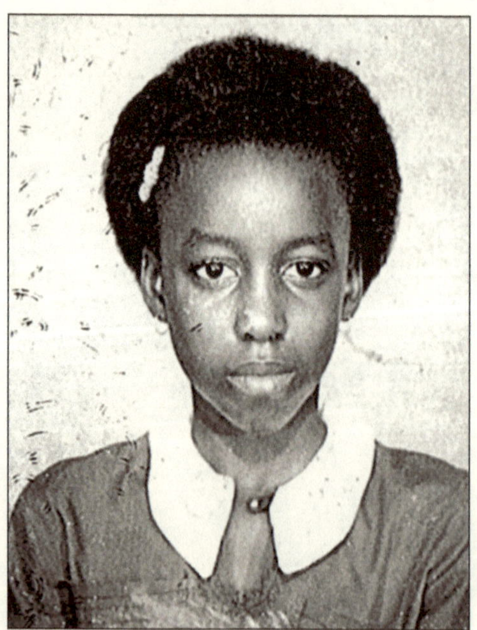

At 10 years old, still in primary school

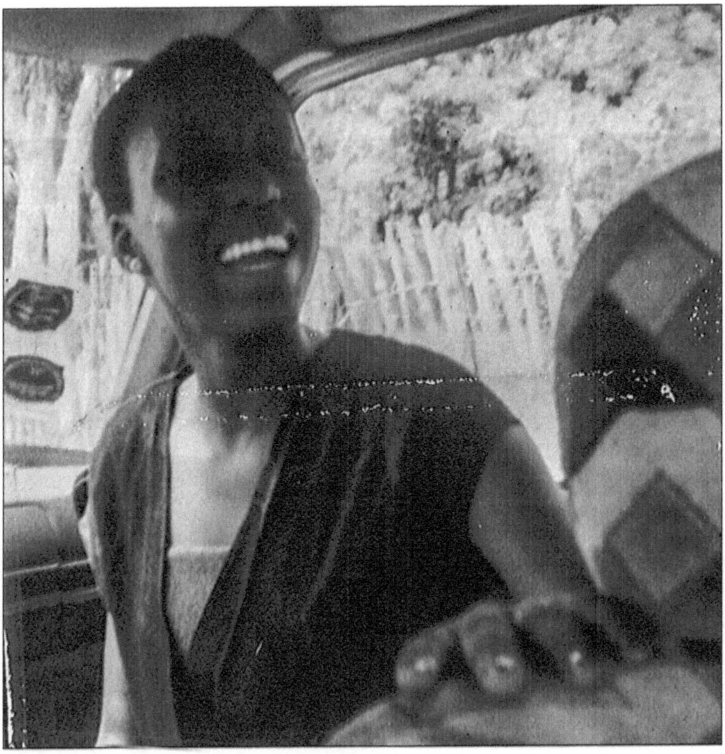

A few months after the haircut incident with Dad

As a young teenager

As a teenager with long and tiny braids

Mum and I on the day I was leaving home as a teenager

Sitting on the chair, from left to right my youngest sister Lu, Dad, Mum, sister Penda. Standing at the back, left to right myself and younger brother Omey. Taken in my parent's house in Seychelles in 1988.

Front entrance of our home in Fajara The Gambia. Front row left to right Penda, Mum, me and Lu. Back row left to right Dad and Omey

As a young chef at Cassio College in the UK

Charles Junior (now Omar) with Linda's children in their home in Leighton Buzzard

Symbolic cooking as part of the wedding rites ceremonial process

On my wedding day with my paternal and maternal grandmothers

With Byes on our wedding night after the traditional rites

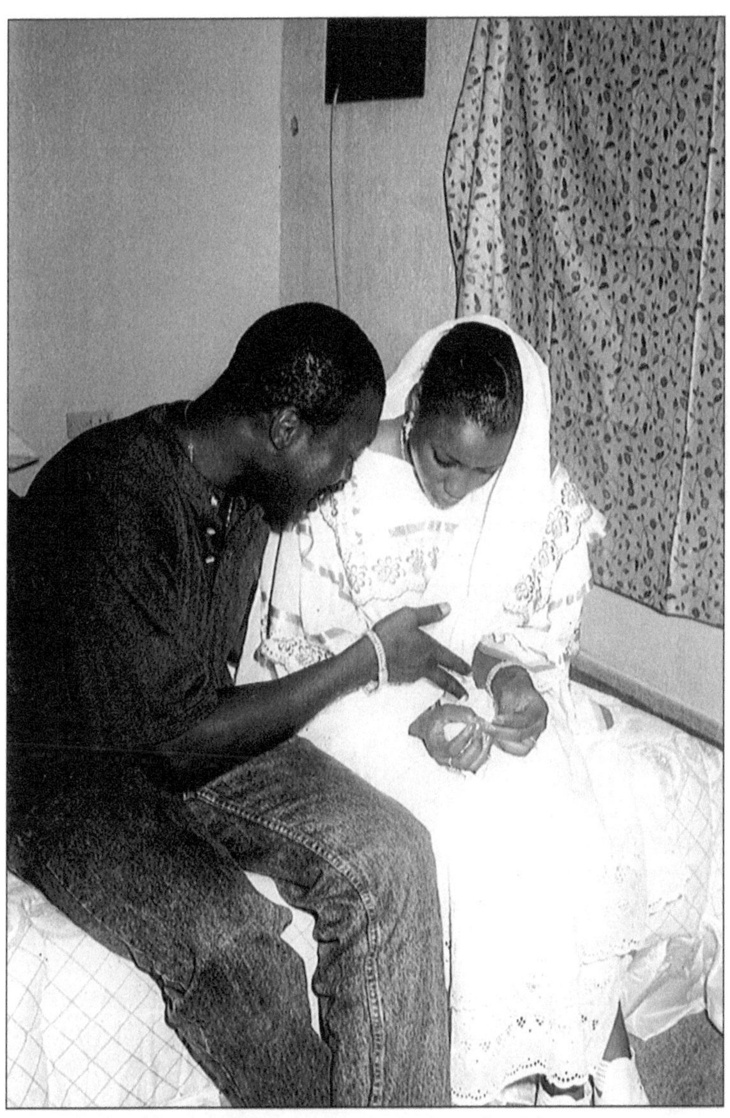

My new husband Byes consoling me when I arrived, emotional, in my new matrimonial home

Graduating with a Masters in Gender Analysis in Development

Byes and I on the day we arrived from Mecca after performing the Hajj

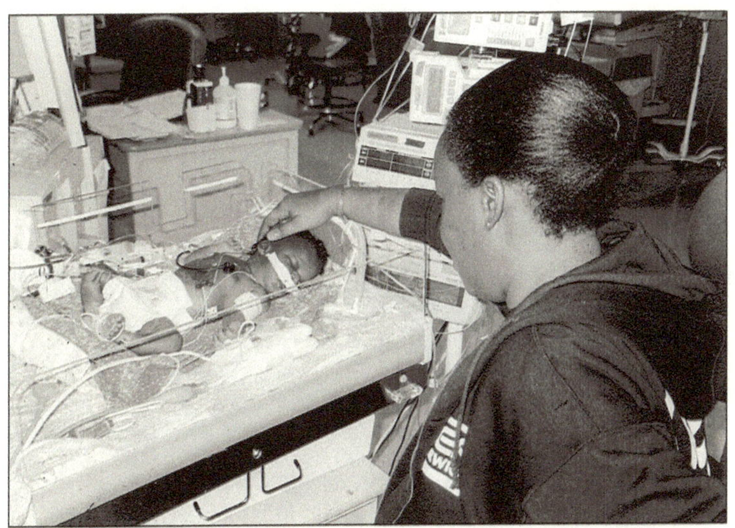

Sitting next to Samsu's cot whilst he was in ICU just after his birth

Family photo taken in 2008, the United Kingdom: from left to right Son Samsu being carried by husband Byes, Byes, daughter Katty, son Mustapha, son Omar and me

Our three older children: Katty, Omar, and
Mustapha in the United Kingdom in 2015

Family photo at daughter Katty's graduation. First Class Honors in Biomedical
Science

Dad and Mum dancing

Television interview on Education
and Information Communications and
Technology (ICT) in Ivory Coast in 2016

Three generations with Mum, myself, and my daughter Katty

Wedding day of eldest son, Omar, with new bride, Mariam

With Arch Bishop Desmond Tutu In 2012
during the Mo Ibrahim Annual Governance
meeting in Senegal

Welcoming Her Excellency Ellen Sirleaf-Johnson, President of Liberia, in Addis
Ababa, Ethiopia during the 50 years anniversary of the Organisation of the African
Union (OAU), recognizing African Women pioneers who contributed to the liberation
for Africa's Independence from colonial rule.

Receiving certificate from President Clinton
on behalf of Forum for African Women
Educationalists (FAWE). Taken in New York
in September 2012, during the Clinton Global
Initiative pledge towards girls' education in
Africa.

With His Excellency Macky Sall, President
of the Republic of Senegal, in 2016,
discussing his role as Lead Champion
Head of State supporting Higher Education
and Scientific Research in Africa at his
Presidential Offices in Dakar, Senegal

With Her Royal Highness Queen Elizabeth II during the Palace
hosting of the Commonwealth Education Fund Programme
reception at Buckingham Palace in London, 2008

Byes and I with H.R.H. Queen Elizabeth II and H.R.H. Prince Philip at CEF palace
reception

With renowned African singer Angelique Kidjo in
New York in 2011, at the launch of the 501-C3
Friends of FAWE

With Mum and Hubby Byes at home in The Gambia, December 2015

With Mum at home in The Gambia in December 2015

With President Adesina of the African Development Bank Group in Seoul, South Korea in 2016, on the Africa/Korea partnership collaboration

www.ingramcontent.com/pod-product-compliance
Lightning Source LLC
Chambersburg PA
CBHW030928060726
47591CB00005B/1705